BEYOND
THE BELL

BEYOND THE BELL

12 Lessons for Navigating Your Life After High School

Melissa Pyrch

Published 2022 by Gildan Media LLC
aka G&D Media
www.GandDmedia.com

FIRST EDITION 2022

Front cover design by Tom McKeveny

Interior design by Meghan Day Healey of Story Horse, LLC

Library of Congress Cataloging-in-Publication Data is available upon request

ISBN: 978-1-7225-0601-8

10   9   8   7   6   5   4   3   2   1

For my students—
let this book be the proof.

Go!

Contents

BEYOND
THE BELL

Objective: Welcome Fear

I wish someone did this for me when I was in high school. I wish someone threw the thematic essays, labs, math equations, and history lessons aside for just one moment and said what all high school kids so desperately need to hear from adults: the truth.

I have tried to do this for my students over the years, but I know there is so much left unsaid. So here they are: the stories that are never told in high school. They are not part of any curriculum map, and no one wants to write them in any textbook. There will be no homework assigned on these chapters. But I assure you there will be a test on this content. Many, many tests. And you will fail. And succeed. And, sadly, no one will grade you harsher than you will grade yourself. That self-evaluation is not even close to who you are and what you can become if you trust yourself and see what I, your teacher, know is inside of you.

Because I am a teacher, your teacher on this journey, I expect you to pay attention. I will not require you to take notes or even highlight these pages. However, I do expect you to put forth your best effort as we go on this journey together lesson by lesson. But first, stop scrolling, and put your phone away, get your earbuds out of your ears, unless of course you are listening to my audiobook, then by all means carry on.

Thank you for your cooperation. Disrespect of any kind will not be tolerated and that includes, most importantly, to yourself. It's okay to doubt yourself and worry about where you are headed while you dive into these pages. However, it's not okay to verbally abuse yourself or bully yourself because you are scared or unsure if you will come out of this place we call high school unscathed.

Put your mind at ease. You will be hurt, you may even shed a few tears over things that matter now, and won't matter later. We all took a few hits in high school. This is all part of this place—the space between. So, head up, helmet on. Head in the game. This book is for you and, selfishly, this book is for me, the high school version of myself that didn't know I'd be brave enough to someday share these stories so real and so raw. I didn't know then that you, my students, would be some of the most important people in my life who would teach me just as much as I've taught you over the years. Perhaps, even more.

Before we go on, I will tell you what my high school self would have loved to hear and what I so desperately want you to know: you are not alone, and everything—and I mean everything—will be okay.

Your "okay" may not look the way you thought it would, and it definitely won't look like anyone else's. Sometimes it might feel like you'll never be okay, and it might feel like the world around you is foggy, dark, and cold as you desperately try to find your way to okay.

Rest assured, this is just fear trying to take over, stop you dead in your tracks, and throw you off your game. Don't fall for it. Instead, welcome fear; in fact, greet your fear with a smile and acknowledge it. After all, you've been here before, right? And you're still here. Hell, you opened this book. You're ready for this journey. Jump in like the younger version of yourself running poolside on a hot summer day screaming, "Cannonball!" Grab both of your knees and hug yourself tightly because there is great joy in jumping into the deep end.

I'm not saying it wouldn't be nice if your diploma came with directions. You know, like a fortune cookie that revealed the secret mission you will embark on after you throw your graduation cap in the air. But growing up doesn't work like that, and, quite frankly, if it did, life would be boring.

Fear of the unknown is extremely motivating. If you are feeling it creep up your back as you look at the sticker price of your top college or if the hair on the back of your neck stands up when you're pressured to click a college major while filling out your college applications, be proud of yourself. These feelings signal that you care so deeply about your future, you are willing to face challenges, stand on fragile ground, and take risks to step into your purpose. Look at anyone you deem as successful and you will find they, too, stood in your shoes.

How do I know? Let me tell you. My parents mortgaged their house to send my brother and me to college. And although I didn't know just how much my parents sacrificed and how much was riding on my college degree, by my junior year in college, I still felt the weight of this four-year journey. I started to see friends decide on specific career paths, and I worried that I would fall behind. The comparison game never ends well. I began to feel irresponsible and embarrassed that I had yet to declare a major. How could I, a future college graduate, finish this endeavor with no career plan? It was unthinkable to me, and I refused to graduate without a résumé that clearly defined my objective.

I did what I always did when I was lost at school: I looked to school for answers and found myself in my college's version of a career counseling center. I felt good walking in there. I felt responsible. It was like I was an archaeologist and I was there to dig up the great secrets of my past and uncover the way to my future. I walked in filled with hope and was excited when I was directed to a computer and told to answer a series of questions. I was told these specific questions would run the gamut, and my answers after they were processed and analyzed would reveal my ideal career.

Perfect, right?

Sudden Death

This test was only going to take about twenty minutes and was exactly what I needed. Twenty minutes. I had spent nearly three years at this college clueless and in twenty minutes this machine was going to figure it all out. Are you kidding me? I was thrilled. I still remember question one: *What do you see yourself wearing to work?* Oh my gosh, I thought to myself, a fashion question? Now we're getting somewhere. I want to dress up of course.

I learned long ago, no one was getting ahead wearing sweatpants to work. All I needed to do was look around my sorority house to figure that out. Sweats all day, done up at night. I still don't really get the dress-down days at work; something seems strange about telling high school seniors to do their homework while sporting Adidas sneakers. Yes, I still wear Adidas original Superstars, new pair, the same style I wore back in college. In fact, I probably had them on the day I took this career test.

Question 2: *Do you like to work with people?* This test was going to work for me, I could feel it. Of course! I was at the pulse of the social scene at college; I was the vice president of a national sorority, and, I will admit, I was rather impressed with myself. I lived with the sorority president and across the hall was the secretary and house president. Huge Greek letters were affixed to the second floor balcony that opened up between our rooms. We would sit out there on warm days, sip cheap beer, and talk about life. None of these titles mean shit now, but at the time, we were killing it. Well, at least that was our version of the story.

After around twenty minutes, just as prom-ised, I waved my hand to signal the counselor who helped to set up the test and eagerly exclaimed, "I'm done!"

"Okay, great. Let's just press submit and print and you can go ahead and pick up your results from the printer." He seemed pretty sure of himself, and it was contagious. I was confident, secure, and excited. This was it. My future was printed, and I was ready to tackle the perfect career designed just for me.

I quickly flipped the paper from the top of the laser printer and scanned the page, my name, date, question responses, and, aha! At the bottom of the page in bold letters, there it stood. Career Sugges-tion: Funeral Director.

This is what my students would now call a WTF moment. I didn't have these words back then, but these are the words I needed. My mouth dropped. My eyes widened, teared, and then burned with anger. I marched back to Mr. Career Counselor and barked, "A funeral director? Is this a joke?"

The next part was the closest I ever came to an actual out-of-body experience. He matter-of-factly, never losing his confidence, grabbed the paper from my hand and said, "Well, let's take a look here."

At this point it was like I was floating above the scene. I hate wakes. I hate funerals. I avoid them at all costs. Growing up, my best friend's grandfather was a funeral director. We would go down to the Bronx to visit him and even sitting in the entrance of the place made me uncomfortable. While our brothers couldn't wait to catch a few gory glimpses down in the basement where they embalmed the bodies, we girls couldn't wait to leave. The smell alone was unbearable: carnations and death. My mind spiraled to these childhood memories as I trembled with terror at the thought of this being my final destination. Pun intended. Then, I was pulled back to the moment.

"Okay. Well, it says here you want to work with people. So—"

"Right. Live ones. Breathing. The people I want to work with, I want to be alive!" This was exactly what I said. Yelled, actually. Through tears, of course, because college sorority girls can be, well, a bit dramatic. And then, I left. I don't remember what that guy looked like; I just know I never saw him again.

I called my mom and repeated the sequence of events: cried, upset my parents, took a shower, got dressed, and partied with my sorority sisters. Not proud, just being honest because that's what I promised you. I don't advise this pattern, but I know there is nothing I can write here that will stop you from being young.

The next day, of course, I went to class. It was a poetry class with one of the coolest professors I ever had. His name was Alex. Dr.? Mr.? A last name? He was too young and too creative for a stuffy title. By allowing us to call him Alex, he was cooler than 100 percent of the educators I have ever met. He was brilliant too. He made the poem *Ode on a Grecian Urn* sound like an intimate exchange we all wanted to see and experience. I vividly recall talking about his class with friends.

I know now that learning and discussion among students after the bell rings is an uncontested sign of an outstanding teacher. I loved this class, just like I loved my high school English class. I left there, like I always did, feeling confident and smart, so I decided it was time once again to face my uncertainty and discomfort about my lack of direction.

It felt like I was on this highway with all these other people, only their GPS had set destinations. I was just driving, aimlessly. Worse, I was afraid I would run out of gas and stall. I couldn't do that to my parents. I wouldn't do that to myself. So, once again, I wandered into the career counseling center, but this time I requested an appointment with an actual person, not a computer, to discuss my future.

There happened to be someone immediately available, so I stepped into her office. She pulled up my transcript and saw the direction I was headed and listened as I told her about my uncertainty as a communications major.

"I want a job after I graduate," I told her. She looked at my grades and saw the abundance of English classes I had successfully completed. She asked about my favorite courses, and I enthusiastically told her about my poetry class with Alex. She asked about high school and peppered me with questions about what I enjoyed most about college, and what type of life I saw myself living after my graduation hat fell to the ground.

More importantly, Mr. Height came to mind. He was my high school English teacher. In his class, I felt like the valedictorian. He taught me how to write. He taught me how to research. I nailed whatever he assigned. I always got an A, which did not come easy to me in other classes. He taught me how to teach too. Although, I had no idea that was happening at the time.

Did you ever stop and think about what is happening to you, for you, right now? You see, there were clues my whole life that teaching English would be my path, but I was so nervous and scared to make the wrong decision that I didn't listen to my gut. I discounted the most important voice in my life: my own. I ignored the copy of the book *Claude the Dog* that my brother bought for me as a child that I adored. I blew off the hours I spent engrossed in Beverly Cleary and Judy Blume novels. I blocked out my dreams of writing a book and the stack of writing journals I always kept next to my bed.

Instead, I listened to others and allowed their versions of teaching cloud my path. Sometimes the voices and ideas of others are necessary and helpful, but your voice should always be the strongest. It's the voice you know best. Trust it.

By this time in our conversation, the answer was clear to this counselor. Confidently, she asked, "Why don't you become a teacher?"

Ugh! I remember the dread I felt. Not again, I thought. I did not have any interest in living out my mother's desire to be an elementary school teacher. I didn't have the patience for little kids, like my mom. I didn't have any interest in puke, wiping noses, or hugging smelly, snotty toddlers.

Don't judge. These were the thoughts of my twenty-year-old self.

I explained these thoughts to the counselor using softer words and she shook her head and laughed. "Not an elementary school teacher. A high school English teacher."

Huh? I thought. And just like that the answer to my future was before me. An answer that, if I had listened, was inside me all along. Most likely, the answer is within you too. How do you find the answer? First, turn up the truth and turn down other people's opinions. This decision is all yours. You're the only one who will have to face the future you create for yourself.

What's Your End Game?

Relax. I get it. Most of you have no idea at this point where your adult self will wind up. But I bet you do know what you enjoy. I bet you know what comes naturally to you, what activities you get lost in, and what feels right.

More importantly, what makes you happy. Almost every move we make is an attempt to move toward what we believe will make us happy. This is what we are all chasing, so do your best to catch it early. I've watched so many kids pursue a path that seemed easy or looked impressive trying to catch an idea of happiness that wasn't right for them.

Matt was a tenth grader who walked around school always meticulously dressed reading business books while everyone else was, well, hardly reading what was required. He was fascinated by big business tycoons who understood the art of negotiation. He was super social and became especially skilled at convincing teachers to let him off the hook for a missed homework assignment, or excusing him when he walked into class a few minutes late. Persuasion became his strong suit.

"Mrs. Pyrch, You don't understand. I'm freaking out. I have a test fourth period and I had to go see my math teacher. I'm sorry. I know I'm late. I know, but I really need to do well on this test. I promise, it won't happen again." He knew it probably would happen again. I knew it definitely would. But even when Matt was overdramatizing an excuse, he was likable and seemed sincere. When he reached out for support or help because he was overwhelmed or stressed, which was often, it was impossible to say no. He had a natural ability to convince people that helping him was the right thing to do.

As I got to know him, it became clear that this kid was a salesman. I still remember telling him, "You could sell sand at the beach." By the time he was a high school senior and approached me to write his college recommendation, I was convinced that advertising and sales were exactly where he was headed. He was not. This is typical. Making this decision at seventeen is too scary and takes time.

Like most of you, he was unsure of where life would take him and afraid to make a mistake. As an early undergrad student, he even attended an informational meeting about the dentistry program at his college. We had a laugh over this as he is the last person who would find joy picking at strangers' teeth. However, it's not unlikely that you will find yourself in strange, sometimes random places, too, as you frantically search for direction. Sometimes it takes one class, one mentor, or even one conversation to find your way.

Just as I suspected, my former student eventually found his way into an advertising class that clicked. He graduated, climbed his way up the corporate ladder, and never turned back. The successful man I know today showed up in my classroom at fifteen years old. The dream career he currently holds selling consumer data to advertisers so they can successfully target digital ads didn't even exist when he left for college. This may be the case for you too. Stay open. It takes time to shed the protective layers that keep us from choosing, especially when the choices seem overwhelming, scary, or don't even exist yet.

You may have moments of sheer terror. If this reality scares you, good. Welcome it. Without fear, you can't find courage. Get ready for a wild, turbulent ride. Hold on and breathe. Chances are you will surprise yourself along the way; I know I did. Who knew? I'm Mrs. Pyrch, your high school English teacher. I'm exactly who I am meant to be.

But this book isn't about me; it's about you. So turn the page and let's explore your next stop on the road to being exactly who you are meant to be.

Objective: Rewrite Your Story

From a young age, you develop relationships with learning and with teachers in a system that in its simplest form is meant to educate you and send you out into the big, wide world to do big important things. On the first day of this journey, many of us experience a similar ritual. Proud parents make sure you are bathed, dressed, and well prepared. This is the day you've been talking about for weeks and everyone is visibly excited. New backpacks are stuffed with properly labeled school supplies and homemade PB&Js. Maybe you wait for a school bus to pull up as *click* the picture is taken to commemorate the moment, and captioned: "First Day of Kindergarten."

Within minutes, social media are flooded with these images, and parents rejoice and text, "Back to School!" Parents today even make kids hold up signs that document the name of the teacher their kids will meet on the other side of the yellow limousine ride; the school bus of course holds promise of the year ahead. It's bumpy, it's fun, it's loud, and there's a lot to learn especially if you sit in the back.

School is promised to be the place where creativity and curiosity are welcomed and dreams are chased. School is a BIG deal. It always has been. It's safe to say that we will forever applaud the start and cheer at the end of one's educational journey.

Here's the problem: this system often labels us, if we let it, as smart, learning disabled, good at math, weak at science, talkative, apathetic, quiet, conscientious, artistic, athletic, a pleasure to have in class, and the list goes on. Teachers write comments on progress reports and report cards four to eight times a year with the best of intentions. These written words and verbal assessments begin to shape you and your academic identity.

These canned comments start happening as early as kindergarten and, damn it, these labels stick. Some labels stick like Post-it notes and fall off easily over time. Some labels feel like badges of honor that you allow to twinkle and shine every time you enter a learning environment. Others stick like the gum left on the bottom of the desks from the beginning of time. Gum that may stay there forever or take a lot of hard work to remove.

From the moment you step foot through the double doors of elementary school and find your first classroom, it begins. Your name is everywhere. Your spaces are labeled in primary colors, and eventually you begin to grow into labels you earned and some you didn't ask for.

I haven't been in elementary school in, let's just say, a very, very long time. Yet, I can still remember so many moments, fleeting for the teacher I'm sure, that stuck with me. Like the time in the first grade during writer's workshop when I approached my teacher's desk and asked her how to spell *TV*. She looked at me sympathetically and said, "T-V."

To which I answered, "Yes. How do you spell it?" She repeated the same two letters, and after a long pause the imaginary lightbulb above my head lit up. Eventually, I caught on, but the embarrassment hung on my shoulders like a wet towel.

You can probably tell a story about your childhood that includes the exact words an adult said that cut to your core. What is the story that hangs around your shoulders? Better yet, how can you let this go or push back against it? The fact is that when you are young, you seek approval from the adults in your life. These adults will have an impact on who you become. Unfortunately, negative messages can be louder than positive messages. I wish this were not true, but often it is.

What to do with such criticism is typically not discussed in classrooms. Even though the lingering effects can be universal. That moment when someone, a teacher, or your parents say or do something that hits at your core, it can trigger emotions that you are even too young to define. This is when most of us meet insecurity and doubt, and, unfortunately, these two tend to stick around.

One of my students recently shared the exact words his third-grade teacher wrote on the top of his writing assignment—an assignment he recalled completing with his mom's help. He was proud of what he handed in, but when his paper returned with his teacher's markings, he saw that she had expressed disappointment and labeled parts of his work as unacceptable. She commented that his work didn't show his true potential as a student. He vividly remembers crying over the exact criticism, *lack of effort,* written in green pen in the margin of a paper he was proud to put his name on.

He was pulled aside in class as his teacher voiced concern that he would always struggle in school. His teacher doubted that he would ever find success as a student. Those words might as well have been tattooed on his chest. These words still haven't disappeared from his memory even though they had been written nearly a decade ago. He was just nine years old at the time.

The critic was a teacher. I would bet her intentions were to encourage him and push him to increase his efforts. But when you are on the receiving end of a message that stings, it's tough to realize the intentions of the sender. You're often stuck taking the hit and sorting through whatever consequences show up later. That same student is about to graduate from college.

Check Your Labels

Here's the thing about school, the tough stuff, the embarrassing moments, the mean teachers, the failing grades, the calls home, the missed questions—these events tend to stick out and stand out. Often, we hang our hats on these moments, and, worse, we start to believe these moments define who we are and what we are capable of. And, moment by moment, lesson by lesson, grade by grade, we come up with a narrative that describes who we are as students and ultimately as people. This then dictates how we handle ourselves in classrooms and how we approach schoolwork and challenges.

As a teacher, I can tell you that even though I try my best to give my students encouragement and confidence, they tell me things like, *I was so afraid of you* or *I thought you were so mean.* Then they explain it was nothing I did, it was just that I held them accountable, or had high expectations for their quality of work.

In other words, regardless of what happens in those thoughtfully decorated classrooms, filled with learning stations, colorful books, and math manipulatives, you will emerge with the exposition of a story, filled with assumptions, and stories, positive and negative, that will serve as the foundation for the chapters to come. I wish I knew the answer to stopping this cycle for you. A cycle we all play a role in that is filled with experiences that shape our academic identities. So what identity have you developed?

A reading teacher pulled me out of class in the second grade because she realized I was in the wrong reading group, and later that week I was moved up to the higher level. This moment is probably why I believed reading and writing were my strengths and the reason I excelled in reading and writing from this point on. Seriously, this moment is when my love for basically what I'm doing right now began.

I fell headfirst into books, filled pages with writing for fun, and was truly excited when the eye doctor said I needed glasses in the second grade. After all, this was the look of a reader and writer. Summer reading? I combed through this list happily and looked forward to finding treasure at our town library. I loved this identity. I believed this story, a story I shaped my life around. These stories are so powerful; they can catapult you forward, but can also hold you back.

At least once a year a kid shows up on my roster who earns an eye roll from his previous teacher at the mere mention of his name. *Oh boy, he's tough. She can be difficult. Nice enough kid, but doesn't do much.* You know these kids from class too. They see no potential in the seat on which they sit.

Justin was one of these kids. He trudged to class every day, uninterested. His clothes were oversized, and he always wore a hat. He carried a backpack filled with crumpled paper that exploded when unzipped. He was easily labeled *apathetic toward academic achievement.* Contrary to what you may believe, many teachers love this type of challenge. If you were one of these kids, you probably know the exact teacher who took you and shook you out of your apathy.

Justin sat in the back of the room and did his best to go unnoticed. Of course, the prime pick for a kid like Justin is in the back of the room behind all of the other kids who fight to sit on the side of the room lined with windows. Typically they are the dreamers. The back of this row doesn't have much of a view, but Justin didn't care.

He struggled to see what was right in front of him anyway. He sat far away from the front where the overachievers plant themselves on day one. He hid from seats closest to the door to avoid the chance of a passing administrator seeing him and pulling him from class for a "talk." The center of the room screams, *call on me!* Sadly, kids like Justin believe they don't have any answers. So he hides. But you really can't hide from a teacher who gets it.

Week after week he would fail quizzes and miss homework assignments. Until the one vocabulary quiz that began the process of changing what felt like a life sentence. That week, the words were manageable and familiar to most students as they started with common prefixes. This was the moment, if he tried, Justin could find success with a little patience and redirection.

"Take everything off your desk except a pen." These words signal the room that an assessment is about to begin. Justin, of course, had nothing to take off his desk and had to ask the annoyed student next to him to borrow a writing utensil. Typical of Justin's routine, he scribbled his name on the top of his quiz, flipped the page over, and immediately put his head down on the cool gray surface of his desktop in a desperate attempt to blend in.

I pulled up a chair next to him and instructed, "Pick up your head." Justin groaned, but he did what I asked.

"You need sixty-five points to pass." He pulled his hat down. It was clear he was bothered by my persistence to get him to try.

"You know what multicolored means, right? So, then, what might it mean to multitask?" He rolled his eyes, reluctantly responded, and wrote in an answer. Together we moved to the next question. He limped through each section of the quiz as I pulled answers from his grasp. This continued until he did enough to earn himself a passing grade.

Look, Justin didn't become the valedictorian, and his total approach to school didn't change overnight, but he was able to prove to himself that he could find success with support and so he began to slowly rewrite his story, and his relationship with school began to shift. This shift can happen in any aspect of your life, if you let it.

What's Holding You Back?

Are you accepting a label that you aren't proud of but you believe you can't shake? If you find yourself at this point, you may be caught in a net of complacency and acceptance. But just because you are caught doesn't mean you can't be set free.

A parent recently wrote, "My daughter is a math and science kid. She dislikes English." The email continued to gush about how, after eleven years of school, she was pleased to hear that her daughter was finally excited about going to English class. Imagine this mother's delight to learn that her daughter was actually reading *The Catcher in the Rye* and enjoying the class discussions.

For years this student was labeled a math and science kid. It became the excuse that justified her reluctance to approach assigned reading, engage in class discussions, and blow off critical essay assignments. It easily explained away a failed quiz or excused a cut class. Her subpar results became accepted and allowed her to stop taking ownership of her performance in English, like being a math and science kid was a hand she was dealt and had to play. Imagine declaring *I'm not a reader* at fourteen years old. It's like saying *I'm a bad driver* when you've only been a back seat passenger. Nevertheless, this story became her truth

You probably have a ridiculous truth too. *I can't dance. I'm not a good artist. I'm just not organized. I'm always late. I can't spell. I suck at writing essays.* I'd bet you've held these statements in your back pocket and pulled them out when needed because it's easier than tackling something challenging. Or quite simply, you may lack any desire to win a spelling bee or enter a dance competition and that's okay.

Unless—you actually want to change something about yourself.

Negative statements, repeated over time, will always be your truth, will hold you back, and place you comfortably in the land of acceptance. The land of acceptance, many times, does not offer a round-trip ticket. Fly there slowly with your eyes wide open. Land the damn plane if you must, but be absolutely sure of what you are willing to accept.

We are taught at birth that the adults around us are there to care for us. In America, we are sent to school at five years old and told to listen to the teacher and do what he or she says. This is the rule. And it is rarely challenged. Most of us hate this idea, so here's how I illustrated our academic culture in my classroom. And I ask you to do this with me now.

Stand up. Raise your right hand. Raise your left hand. Put both hands on your head. Repeat after me: "Why am I doing this?" Now sit down.

If you did this exercise like my seniors do every year, you'd see me throw my hand up in the air and ask, "Why did you just do all of that?" Their answer was quick and simple: "Because you asked us to."

Why did you do it? Because I asked you to?

That was it. I knew it. They knew it. They said they hoped I was going to make a point. They have come to expect this from me. I give them questions or activities and together we find the big ideas that apply to whatever text we are examining. They were right this time too. I was showing them the behaviors they have adopted as learners. This started twelve years ago when they walked into a kindergarten classroom, and old habits can be difficult to break.

Most likely, adults, who are right this exact moment working on their doctorates, are listening to teachers and doing what they say. But what if a teacher says something awful? What if the adult tells you something about yourself that you can't unhear or refuse to accept?

You get to push back. You get to reject criticism. Better yet, you are allowed to take criticism, evaluate the critic, and consider its value to you and your life. I'm not saying that you should walk through life or your academic journey with a chip on your shoulder, but you absolutely get to choose which criticisms will lead you to progress.

If you see yourself in that little boy whose confidence was lanced with a green pen or you have been labeled with harsh words, or used your weakness as an excuse, you still get to decide whether you want to continue to live in that unfavorable space. If you've learned to give up and meet the low expectations of critics around you, let me be clear: you've given your power away. It's a choice to cosign the negative thoughts in your head about what you can and cannot achieve. Can you find the strength to overcome the nonsense that slithered its way into your story? Do you have faith in yourself?

Self-doubt is rough. It rears its ugly head at the worst times. During the times when what you really need is confidence, self-doubt tends to take over. Maybe you have been labeled or have decided what your strengths are, but don't let this left brain/right brain labeling limit you.

Yes. I slayed my English classes. It was in these classes that I fine-tuned my critical writing skills. It was in these spaces that taught me the methods I would someday teach my own students. I didn't know it then, but every red A that sailed onto my desk reinforced that I excelled in reading and writing. Research paper? Yes, please. I had no fear because being a strong writer was in my fabric. That's what I was told in the second grade and here I am: writing this book.

Use Your Delete Key

How about you? The challenges life throws are easy to identify. Taking them on and facing them feels worse than a video game that levels up in difficulty every time you pass a checkpoint. But what's your power up? What contribution are you ready to share with the people in your life who never doubted you? It's important to note that these supportive people are most likely all around you just waiting for you to realize your potential. I'm waiting too.

Tackling a challenge and proving to yourself that you can be successful will allow you to shed any label you think you have been forced to carry in high school. It might not always feel like it, but you are always in charge of your own identity. Replace the labels with a new reality so you can proudly say *I earned an A* or *I wrote a winning essay* or *I got accepted into grad school*. This is the beauty of your story. You have a delete key and get to make edits any time you want. Never forget. You, and only you, are the writer of your story.

Lesson 3

Objective: Start at the Beginning

High school can be like this: One day you're a freshman; you're a frog hopping across a four-lane highway looking up at a bunch of upperclassmen who look secure and cool. You walk through the halls and wonder if you'll ever have that senior-year swagger.

Then, in a blink, you're an upperclassman wearing a brand new T-shirt you picked up at a college bookstore during an open house your mom set up. You walk through the last days of your senior year wondering if anyone can tell you're shitting your pants at the thought of leaving your hometown and being seen as an actual adult.

When the time comes to leave home and take that plane ride or long drive in your parents' SUV, stuffed with all the crap on that list you were told you *had* to buy for college or else you might as well give up now, it might feel like you are on a pirate ship battling the rough seas. It could go either way: Maybe you feel like a prisoner, blindfolded, and forced to walk the plank. Or, Captain, you are ready and excited for a crazy adventure with a bunch of spirited friends looking for treasure.

Either way, once you're on that ship, you have to set sail. I, for one, felt seasick. My parents had to pull over several times because I warned them I wasn't feeling well; I was a nervous wreck.

Needless to say, I got over it and you will too. My second semester roommate, yes, you can always change roommates, later my sorority's president, quickly became one of my best friends. She gifted me her older sister's ID, which made us related on paper, and just like that the four-year adventure began. She also handed me my first plastic cup, filled it with cheap draft beer, and stood by me as we widened our circle of friends—extended family actually—for the next four years.

Like most college freshmen, you will cling to the people who live on your dorm floor. You will find comfort in the fact that you are all trying to navigate the first few weeks of being on your own, and hopefully you will find fast friends. Your dorm room, adorned with fading high school memories, will quickly fill with new experiences. It won't take long to see the lesson play out that you have to live to learn.

The place you call home can change. It's a state of mind. Home is a place where you can rest easy and be raw with people who take hold of you like family. Sometimes leaving the physical place you've always known will finally give you the room you need to grow without limitations. It's human nature to desire safety, security, and love. Embracing this new beginning filled with new people and experiences will, if you let it, guide you comfortably to a new home.

Former students of mine stop by their "old" high school during their first fall breaks, or show up at the homecoming game to show off worn college sweatshirts or newly earned Greek letters and report similar starts. *I switched roommates. My roommate is awesome. I might transfer. My anthropology, sociology, geology (insert any –ology here) class is impossible! The food is terrible. I love it. I'm so happy.*

These statements are typical and often all over the place, but the excitement and uncertainty of freshman year is universal and will catapult you through the next four years. Just like it did in high school.

Unless of course you jump right into the work force. These are typically the same kids who declared, "I don't need to write a college essay, I'm not going to college." When pushed or questioned, most were eager to have more time to grow businesses they started while sitting in high school classrooms. Some, already learning a trade, or content with continuing to learn how to run a family-owned business, craved the freedom to concentrate their efforts on the future they had already mapped out.

Or you find yourself dedicated to the military. For some, this is a calling that can't be ignored. This is the case for many of my students like one who sat in my classroom senior year and declared, "I think I'm going to be a marine."

Between his brother's influence as a member of the military himself, and his own desire to give back to his country, my student eventually knew this was a decision that would forever make him proud.

Nevertheless, whatever path you choose, high school becomes a landmark that becomes smaller and smaller in the rearview.

Fall break or Thanksgiving eve is usually the last time I see former students at their "old" high school, if at all. Because high school fades and often doesn't serve them anymore. You will outgrow high school too. It easily slips behind the importance of the present and the thrill of what's next.

At the end of those four fast post–high school years, you will graduate and you may head back to your hometown that strangely doesn't feel the same anymore. Hell, you might even be right back in the bedroom you grew up in. Everything in that space may be exactly the way you left it. High school pictures displayed, dusty old soccer trophies, and other childhood memorabilia like your favorite stuffed toy might still decorate the space. The greatest change however just might be that the person who grew up there is, well, all grown up.

As the college graduation parties commence and the ink dries on your greatest academic accomplishment to date—your diploma—once again, you will find yourself at the beginning. At the beginning there is nothing left to do but start. Relax.

You've been here before. Welcome back to a familiar place with a new perspective. This is growth.

Who Wouldn't Want You?

This time, you have a résumé. A shitty one perhaps, but at twenty-two years old with a bachelor's degree in hand and a list of possible job experiences like camp counselor, lifeguard, retail employee, cashier, landscaper, barista, pizza delivery driver, or maybe an internship in your field, you are puffed up and ready to go for it. Your résumé might show your involvement in philanthropic events or your membership in a national organization. Who wouldn't want you?

Leave out perhaps your ability to stay up all night to finish a paper or cram for a test. There's no reason to mention the class you dropped because you couldn't get up at 8:00 a.m. Definitely don't brag about your involvement in college parties like keg-offs or Greek initiation ceremonies. Nobody needs to know that the cup you are holding on social media has been filled more times than you can remember.

Side note: Please don't let your social media presence hinder your new beginning. Clean that up if you must, but I am going to assume here that your brain already understands the consequences of your digital footprint. Your future employer will Google you. This is a fact. If you're reading this thinking, *I'm going to own my own business,* great. Your clients, customers, and competition will Google you too. Clean it up. Put a little elbow grease into it if need be, but don't let a silly picture discredit who you really want to be.

Your résumé should be polished and clean and your references available upon request. At this point, you are ready to post it on the best professional platforms so employers in your field of expertise can find you. Can't you just see it? Your résumé will be opened like a digital present by your dream employer. What luck that your résumé landed on his or her desk? The calls will roll in, the interviews will be a snap, and really the biggest obstacle will be choosing the best offer with the most money, and the nicest facility. A reasonable commute and excellent health benefits are a given of course.

Delusion. I always loved it. Still do. It's a wonderful place of comfort and joy. The reality is my own and the facts are optional. I actually love the state of delusion so much that I'm shocked when I get an email notifying me that one of my students is suspended for vaping or verbally abusing another teacher. In my mind, all my students are respect-ful and kind. Like I said, I have a huge ocean-front house in the beautiful state of Delusion. Feel free to visit anytime. This is where I was living as I pictured my résumé sailing out into the world of education and onto the desks of administrators.

I guess when you grow up being taught that if you do the right thing, even if it's the hard thing to do, you will be rewarded. You just assume life will offer up what you've worked hard to obtain. In my case, this meant that I would easily land a teach-ing job. News flash: life doesn't work that way. Nevertheless, as my friends were slowly finding their ways through the post-college storm, it never occurred to me that while they were accepting entry-level jobs, teaching assistant jobs, and per-manent sub positions that I would have to settle for a not-quite-right job too.

Two of my closest friends graduated with degrees in health science and health administra-tion. Tara never missed a class. She was smart, mature, meticulous, and diligent and had aspira-tions of running a hospital or even being a county health executive, like her financially successful aunt. As Tara started her job search, she found herself working at a health insurance company. That job didn't fulfill her résumé objective, but it was a job somewhat related to her field. She signed with this company, grabbed some mature looking clothes from Ann Taylor at the mall, and declared, "You gotta start somewhere."

Stacy had a similar career goal as Tara did and wound up working in the credentialing department of a company that provided vision care benefits. Who knows what she actually did at that job, but she had access to great sunglasses.

Joe earned a degree in biology from a state school. He always loved science, but had no idea what to do with his diploma. Shortly after graduation he decided to sign up and take the police test just to see how he would do. Turns out, he scored well and made the top of the list, conquered the physical test, blew through the academy, and just started his career as an officer. Who knew?

Another one of my former students graduated from Alabama's Fashion Institute of Technology with a degree in design, but she found herself aspiring to be a buyer for a major retailer. After graduation, she continued to accept jobs in sales, the field she had worked in since she was sixteen, hoping to learn and climb the corporate ladder. Her first jobs led her to selling retail at luxury brands like Louis Vuitton. She just admitted, "I actually don't know what I want to do."

Another friend of mine, Krista, outgoing, fun, super smart, graduated from Loyola with a degree in speech pathology and accepted her first job post college at a toy company. That job had absolutely nothing to do with her degree, but she did get to travel to Hong Kong that year.

What the hell? Right? But you don't want to miss this. Starter jobs are experiences. Experiences that delete the nonsense from your résumé and add new skills to what you already have to offer and help you figure out how to sharpen or alter your actual professional goals.

How did I miss this? I dismissed the starter jobs my friends were accepting and continued to wait for my full-time teaching job with full benefits to find me. It never occurred to me that I wouldn't be teaching the September after graduation. I mean, come on! I had a degree, for God's sake, and a résumé. It took a few weeks of radio silence to kick me out of delusion. Reality was knocking at my door, and reality does not like to be ignored.

See, this is the thing about college that you have to understand. The fantasy is that college is supposed to educate you right into a career with growth potential that will eventually help you to support yourself and make it on your own. Don't get me wrong, this does happen for some college graduates. However, this degree is not a guarantee that you will slide right into the career that you believe you are ready to start. It's just one "degree" above high school, and let me tell you, you don't get to sit back, relax, and wait for the opportunities to present themselves.

You will be inexperienced and you will be a risky choice for an employer. Even if you want to launch your own business, you have to be willing to push yourself, seize every opportunity to gain new experiences, and stand out. Why? Because you are going to sail around in a sea filled with college degrees and various work experiences looking for land. Often it takes time before the wind hits your sail just right. Are you willing to explore?

Part of exploring simply requires you to go on interviews and reach out to people who may help you get closer to what you truly want in your professional life. In other words, you have to be willing to hustle. If you've made it this far and do not have any work experience under your belt, starter jobs are not only helpful for you, they might be necessary. These jobs help flex your work ethic and challenge you to work with people you otherwise wouldn't know doing tasks you didn't know you could do.

I was twelve years old when I started to earn my first paycheck. A friend of mine and I worked as phone solicitors for a lawn company. True. I knew nothing about taking care of lawns, but I learned to use my personality to sell lawn evaluations to suburban homeowners. At twelve years old, I learned I wasn't so shy after all. Random. I know, but every experience informs you of your next move.

My nephew Sal landed his first job as a lifeguard at a private camp at sixteen years old. The pay was less than minimum wage, and he fought back when his father insisted that he spend his summer working. Sal, who has always been motivated by money, didn't understand the point of working at a job that paid less than he could make working at a fast-food restaurant.

Sal lost the argument. His father signed him up for a lifeguard course. Sal passed the required swim test and was quickly asked to work overtime shifts. Surprisingly, midsummer Sal found himself fully committed to his new job. He was sun-kissed, swam every day, and was happy to have made a bunch of new friends. By the end of the summer, Sal was talking about the opportunities available to him for next season as a result of his new work experience—an experience he tried to avoid.

If you don't go, you'll never know. Step boldly out of your comfort zone even if every fiber of your being would rather jump back in bed and hide under your blankets that smell like your mom just washed them. I'm rolling my eyes, you should know. Sure. The beginning can be hard, but there is nowhere else to start.

My first interview for a full-time teaching position finally came midsummer after my college graduation. At twenty-two, this sorority girl's first thought was, of course, *What should I wear?* I wish I were trying to be funny here, but this is the honest truth. I was that clueless. I'm telling you this because you probably are too. And you don't know it; I didn't either. Keep it moving. You, too, will laugh at yourself later.

In defense of concerning yourself with your appearance when you start interviewing, you should know that I teach in my public speaking class that appearances do matter when you first meet someone. This of course applies to interviews as well. If you present yourself in an unappealing way, guess what? You will not appeal to the audience.

Today we live in a world where saying this is not a popular opinion. I agree. It would be nice if looks didn't matter, but showing up wearing your favorite jeans or, worse, ripped jeans, Adidas Superstars, and a camo long-sleeved T-shirt doesn't say professional. It just doesn't. Sorry, not sorry. Another amusing phrase my students taught me. Sometimes, the words of teenagers are exactly what you need as an adult. Like I said, I learn from them every day.

I wore a floral two-piece skirt and top, a matching set, that I wouldn't be caught dead in anywhere else but at this interview. I can't believe it now, but that's all I did to prepare for my first interview. No work bag, no examples of lesson plans, no student work to show. Just me, in my hideous outfit and my inspired-by-Gucci crossbody bag. Go ahead, you can roll your eyes. I can take it. And, quite frankly, I deserve it.

Without getting into the details, I mean do you really need them at this point? I blew it. The most humiliating part of the interview was my answer to the simple question: *What do you enjoy reading?*

Now, remember, I am trying to score a job as an English teacher. How did I not see this question coming? The school administrator might as well have asked me the square root of 710,114. My reaction was the same. *Hmm. Um.* I may have even looked up and around the room like I was searching for some obscure title.

When I finally blurted out an answer, I said, "I like reading about current events. You know, like the newspaper." I am literally squirming as I write this. I was twenty-two. Do you really think I sat down at my parents' kitchen table with a cup of coffee and flipped through the *New York Times* on a daily basis? I wouldn't even do that now. But that's what I said. That was the answer that I said to a panel of professional educators.

I wish I did what I have told my public speaking students to do when they have to field a question that might be difficult to answer. This is a process you should also review before going on any interview. Turn the question into a statement, start talking, provide specific examples to illustrate your point, and be honest. I could have easily said that with the demands of college, the last book I read was a young adult piece titled *My Side of the Mountain* because I was asked to work with this text while student teaching. I could have also mentioned my love for Tim O'Brien's book, *The Things They Carried*.

Beach reads, chick lit, classic lit, poetry, young adult literature, cookbooks—for the love of God, any of these categories would have worked. Can you tell I have answered this question in my head a million times? But, at the time, my unprepared, green, inexperienced self drew a complete blank. You may struggle during the interview process, too, especially if you don't consider what you want to share about yourself, your experiences, or your love for the field you want to work in.

Anything would have been better than the ridiculous lie I told. Looking back, it was a lie that I felt I needed to tell. You may fall into this trap too. Trying to show up as who you think they want, not as who you are with what you have to offer, will never work. Sure, you can walk into that interview as an image of what you think a professional in your desired field looks like, but make sure you back up the image with preparation and confidence in yourself and your ability to work hard, be open-minded, and willing to learn.

That interview kicked my ego's ass. Sometimes that's exactly what you need to remind yourself that your résumé, desire, and degree mean nothing if you don't intend to keep getting better and continue working toward your goals even when it's hard.

The summer passed and I did get several more opportunities to interview, and question by question, I did get better. I started to bring my student teaching portfolio with me, and if I got stuck, I pulled some sample lesson plans or student work from my bag. I also worked on some canned responses to typical interview questions.

You should too. Although you may have seen similar questions when you first applied to college, your answers should show how far you've come. Treat the interview process like a great opportunity to showcase who you are. Remember, the people interviewing want you to be great. They want you to get the job, mainly so they can go home and don't have to stay late to keep interviewing people.

Interviewing for "the job" that you are working toward every time you take on a project at school, show up to class, or consider internship opportunities may feel worlds away. Until it's not and you're sitting across from people who can change your life with one offer.

Be Ready

What are your strengths? What do you enjoy doing in your free time? Why our school/company/branch? Tell us about a challenge you overcame. Although you will get better as you go, the simple fact you have no control over will remain: You are young and inexperienced, and it may show. So be humble. Ask questions. Be grateful to be part of the process and for every opportunity that comes your way. The right one will show itself.

How do I know? I was fortunate to land an interview at a high school known to be a diverse place;

kids either lived in mansions, found themselves in gangs, slipped through the cracks, or filled the spaces between. Believe it or not, this is exactly the type of challenge and school community I wanted to be a part of. I had thoughts of grandeur even back then and believed, like I do now, that anyone can do anything if he or she has the right role model. These were the clients I wanted.

When the interview started, I was feeling positive. You will know when you start to feel comfortable in an interview. You'll feel the floor under your feet and be able to focus on the people across the table from you. You will feel present and secure in your answers. The questions will feel like softballs being thrown at you instead of sharp, piercing darts like this one: "So, obviously you're young. How would you handle a student making an inappropriate advance?"

Your stomach may drop. But once a question is asked, once the dart is thrown, you have no choice but to respond. I took a deep breath, adjusted in my seat, and looked her straight in her eyes: "Well, I can't imagine this being a problem. There would be no reason for one of my students to feel comfortable crossing the distinct line between teacher and friend. My students will see me as their teacher, and their teacher only. I have no intention of making friends or inviting any inappropriate behavior regardless of my age. If a student dared to cross this line, I assure you, it would be made abundantly clear that this should and will never happen again."

Tough questions will always exist at the beginning of any endeavor. Speak the truth. Your truth. Although your confidence may be fragile, and your experience is light, never doubt who you are at your core. Your values can push you through every obstacle you encounter.

I am telling you about this moment because you need to know that no one should make judgments about you based on your age. Any age. No one should think you have nothing to offer because they are older or younger than you. I learn from my students every single day, but I also learn from my more experienced colleagues, and my peers. Everyone, and I mean everyone, has something to offer. That's a fact. And so are these: Alexander Graham Bell received a patent for the telephone at twenty-nine. Lorraine Hansberry wrote *A Raisin in the Sun* at twenty-six. Do we even need to talk about twenty-three-year-old Mark Zuckerberg? Age is a nonentity. I proved that fact to myself that day.

A week later, the assistant principal called to say they went with a more experienced candidate.

It stung. But that interview, that experience, was a defining moment in my job search. You will have these defining moments too. You will grow each time you find yourself at the beginning and your confidence will grow too. You will start doing well, especially when you show up as the professional version of yourself. It's that simple.

The entry-level jobs, the low-paying job you're not sure is worth your time, the strange job that has nothing to do with the degree you earned, all have a purpose. Embrace an alternative to what you expected while you continue to look for new beginnings. This life can be unpredictable.

That assistant principal who rejected me just a few weeks earlier reached out to me the day before the first day of school. Turned out, they had a late retiree and were short one English teacher. Just like that I found myself at the starting line—again. You will too. You will leave your familiar childhood bedroom, unsure of what tomorrow will hold with nothing left to do but step forward with hope that whatever new experience comes your way, it will place you at a beginning that will lead you to an unexpected place you can someday call home.

Lesson 4

Objective: Make Mistakes

No matter what job you take or what profession you choose, on your first day you are as green as a Granny Smith. Forgive the apple reference, but I can't resist. You are new and shiny and you may stand out in a barrel of Red Delicious. The first day can be brutal. It may test everything you've learned and leave you physically and mentally exhausted. You won't have all the answers and that's okay. Nobody does.

They say "2 teach is 2 touch lives 4ever." I know they say this because I had a keychain that declared it. It was written on a black piece of wood in white writing with a little red apple resting on the corner. It was supposed to look like a chalkboard with a math equation scribbled on its surface. I may have had this dangling from my car keys, but it's too embarrassing to confirm. My first day of teaching went nothing like that keychain promised it would. I'm sure I didn't touch many lives that day, and I'm hoping if I did, none of it lasted forever.

The first day of school: this time, for the first time I was the teacher. *The teacher.* It's funny, when you land a job, all of a sudden you are supposed to identify with this new title. Meanwhile, deep down you're hoping no one asks a question that throws a blinding floodlight on your lack of experience and knowledge of what's supposed to be your field.

I believe this is true no matter what profession you find yourself in. I mean, I can't imagine Dr. Whoever knows every cure to every ailment that walks in her office on the first day she starts at the clinic. Or how could a brand new lawyer possibly know every layer to every law? There is a reason these offices are filled with shelves stocked with books. Right?

Or how about a start-up company, where the rules are just being created, the staff is new, and the risk is high. Most of us have been part of these first days and have seen big mistakes in action.

First days happen in every field, everywhere, and often these first days aren't pretty.

A brand new barbecue place that opened up in the middle of a hot spot about a half hour outside of Manhattan was the perfect location for a new restaurant. The two young guys in managerial positions were ready and excited to make this place the newest hangout for families grabbing dinner and young people looking to unwind with drinks after work.

These two guys were friends: one, in his mid-thirties, a little bit cocky about his experience in the restaurant business, had managed successful restaurants before, and the other, well, he was a nice guy who was understanding to all of the employees starting out and willing to put in the work to train people, most of whom had zero experience.

These two guys trained a group of over fifteen people to be on their waitstaff. Some were also trained to bus tables and run food. Everything seemed to be in order after weeks of preparation, so the owner and the two managers decided it was time for a soft opening. Issues were quickly revealed. Food orders for an entire table, which should have been ready at the same time, haphazardly left the kitchen. Servers forgot to place drinks on trays and were caught carrying them by hand, and many servers offered complimentary baskets of homemade chips before taking orders. This mistake, left uncorrected, can easily decimate food orders and result in a decrease of overall sales.

It was no one's fault; mistakes happen when people are thrown in new situations. Most of the time, a lot has to be learned in a short amount of time because time is money. Tables needed to be turned over quickly, because this location was not cheap. When the restaurant opened at full capacity, many more issues rose to the surface. Dinner shifts were chaotic, and, as expected, the place was packed with hungry people of all ages. The phone rang incessantly with people requesting large pick-up orders. This left diners sitting at tables and people waiting for carryout orders that were way behind schedule. Have you ever had to deal with a crowd of h-angry people?

That first night, the wait staff left there smelling like barbecued meat, with sauce on their logo T-shirts, crumpled cash in their pockets, and throbbing feet. It was a typical start filled with missteps and an overload of new information for how to do better and work smarter next round. If you've entered the workforce, you probably have a story about your experiences at work, the mistakes you made, and most importantly what you learned.

This is cringeworthy, but stay with me on this. I wore a purple suit on my first day as a teacher. Yes. You read that correctly. I wore a purple suit. It was deep purple, let's call it plum. It was a skirt and blazer set. I twisted my hair up and carried a black leather attaché case. I loaded that case with new pens, sharpened pencils, highlighters, a folder, and my binder filled with lesson plans from student teaching. I must have looked like an eggplant, carrying a briefcase, going to work that day. That suit was my professional armor. That case was my shield. But they weren't enough.

Let's Get Ready to Fumble

You see, you'll never have everything you need when you are first starting out, and that especially includes knowledge in the field. It's best to prepare your mindset and get ready to learn from the mistakes coming your way rather than to worry about being the perfect teacher, nurse, entrepreneur, manager, doctor, lawyer, mason, critic, broadcaster, fireman, plumber, soldier, accountant, or [fill in your dream profession]. You will not be perfect, and that's where you will find beauty in your new role.

Many times, it can be a blessing to be the one in the room who is young and naive. When you don't even know what you are supposed to be concerned with, it's easy to walk blindly forward. In simple terms: ignorance is bliss. I definitely didn't know exactly what I was walking into. My schedule indicated that I had a study hall first period. Perfect, I thought to myself. This will give me a few minutes to breathe and review my plans for the day. Wrong.

Get used to it—being wrong, that is. This is the nature of new experiences.

Sarah, one of my seniors, a shy, conscientious student, started her first job the summer before her senior year. She thought working as a lifeguard with her best friend would be a great way to enter the workforce. She landed what she thought would be an easy gig working at a nearby country club. That first day Sarah arrived a half hour early ready to go. She greeted a few of the other staff members, then climbed up to her perch, and began her first shift in the lifeguard chair. It was a sunny July day, and a perfect breeze kissed the water every few minutes. As she adjusted her sunglasses she thought to herself, *How hard could this be?*

She quickly noticed a little girl about three years old taking off her puddle jumper, the flotation device she was using to help her stay afloat, and whining, "I don't want it!" Her mother tried to wrestle it back on her daughter, but there was no fighting it. The little girl insisted on staying in the water and picked Sarah's first day to learn how to swim.

Sarah watched as the little girl played on the steps of the pool and did her best to doggy paddle around the shallow end. Sarah's heart was in her throat for the next thirty minutes as her eyes darted around the pool, paying close attention to the little girl trying to swim for the first time, while also making sure the rest of the swimmers were safe.

Sarah was lucky that day to have coworkers reassure her that the little girl was safe the whole time, and she did a great job overseeing this tricky situation. A tricky situation she didn't see coming, but handled.

That study hall I was up against on my first day was packed with over a hundred students. I looked at the list and it was spinning with names like Jose, Luis, Janelle, Damien, Jose, Luis, Janelle, and Damien. Correct. I had to call their last names too. For those of you who have ever sat in any classroom, on either side of roll call, you know this is teacher suicide. The teacher is uncomfortable, the class is ready to snicker at any mispronunciation, and the teacher's credibility is lost in those five minutes. And everyone knows, there is no choice.

The teacher must jump into this pit of snapping alligators because taking attendance is state law. So I jumped. And you will, too, because you will be up against a moment you waited for that looks different from the scenario you pictured, and you will make mistakes that won't destroy you or your will to succeed.

After the second bell rang to start class, I started to take attendance. I mispronounced names. More accurately, I butchered names, and kids raised eyebrows, rolled eyes, and giggled. I realized by the end of the list I was laughing too. When I called Mayra and pronounced it MAY-ra not My-ra, I was met with a serious attitude and pure disgust as this tenth grader corrected me. I turned to her and said, "Well, I just figured maybe you'd want to try something new this year, but okay if you want to stick with MY-ra. That's fine." She broke her snarl and smiled; we all did. I made a phonetic note near her name and a mental note in my head that I was going to be okay.

It was at this moment that I learned my sense of humor would serve me well, and in this profession it would be everything. What do you have to offer? What parts of your personality have helped you overcome new challenges in the past? Don't be afraid to show your authentic self. Most likely this uniqueness will help you shine, even when you are fumbling through your first experiences.

Play the Field

Making mistakes may not be comfortable for you at first. You may hate feeling vulnerable as a neophyte in this new position. I know I did. It's not easy trying to walk confidently in your new role when you may doubt you're even able to stand. That purple suit sure didn't help either. Like most new professionals, you'll find yourself trying various approaches to solve problems; you'll compare yourself to your established colleagues; you'll lie awake at night trying to understand why the day didn't go as planned; you'll have internal struggles about what you should do, and what you want to do; and you'll throw a shitload of creative ideas out into the world to try and figure out what works.

It's no secret most teachers, most professionals, are standing on a floor covered in shit that didn't work. As a student, I bet you've seen tons of shit too. These are the many mistakes that lead to the good stuff. The experts in any profession usually have countless bad days, missed marks, and false starts. For me, the bell kept ringing, so I had no choice but to keep trying.

One day, during that first year, I was teaching *Julius Caesar* to a class packed with tenth graders. I was reviewing Mark Antony's famous funeral speech, you know the one, "Friends, Romans, countrymen, lend me your ears." I was defining ethos, pathos, and logos. Honestly, I was killing it up there.

And then, a hand went up. I can still see his face; Diego had chiseled features, brown eyes, slick black hair, and wore a cross earring that dangled from his right ear. I remember this student so vividly because weeks before, when he wasn't in class, and the daily attendance came back from the office, his name had a J next to it. I asked the truant officer in our building what this code meant. There were so many letters to remember: A-absent, I-illegal absence, E-excused absence, C-cut, V-vacation, and the list went on. He explained this student had to deal with a slight legal issue, and J indicated jail/juvenile hall.

Upon his return, this student also asked me to sign a form for his probation officer to vouch for his attendance in my class. I never did learn what exactly was the issue, but I liked this kid. He was kind to me, and funny, and despite clear issues with his behavior, I think he had a shot at doing great things in life. I spent my whole career rooting for the kids others doubt. So when his hand went up, it felt like a victory.

And then, I called on him. He stumbled to say, "Ah Ms., you are twenty-two? So, like, can you buy beer?"

Ugh. It was like someone peed on my charcoal. Thanks to my dad for that expression; it's the only simile that comes to mind here. Seriously, this question deflated my teaching high. The rest of the kids couldn't help but giggle as I rolled my eyes and kept right on teaching.

Truth be told, this question taught me something worth remembering. As a teacher, as a person, what you are throwing out in your new space may not be received the way you hoped. It doesn't mean you shouldn't do it, try it, or say it, because when the *it* does go as planned or even better, it makes all the mistakes worth it. That year, I made many, many mistakes.

Thankfully, I also learned how to collaborate with my colleagues. It was those educators who really showed me how to be a teacher. And when the kids were not in the room and the faculty room door was closed, they taught me to have fun and laugh at work. Laughter is what I loved most about those English teachers who took me under their wings and helped me navigate through my first year of teaching.

You will never forget the people you are lucky to learn from while making mistakes at your first attempt stepping into a new career. Aspire to be one of these people. Nothing compares to being out in the field, and the field is a little smaller and less lonely with colleagues who want you to succeed and believe in your potential.

Most people are more inclined to hire those with experience because it is, often times, a safer choice. If you start a job and you're not willing to ask questions, be vulnerable, and learn from the experts, you are a loose cannon. And we all know what can happen with a loose cannon. You do not want your ego to get in your way during your first year at any job. Stand back. Observe. Learn. Try. Fail. Succeed. You will be better for it.

I learned more that year than I did in almost two years of education classes. Because even though I am a proud veteran teacher, it's true: the college classroom can't prepare you for the unexpected. There will be moments that leave you saying, "You can't make this up." Sure. You can talk about it and consider all sorts of scenarios, but when life presents the unexpected, all you can do is step up to the plate and take a swing.

That year, I didn't know what was coming. I learned about the local gangs, their signs, and colors. I learned some of my dear students were gang members and they didn't scare me. I learned to love them and see them as desperate kids who showed up to school because school was safe. I learned how to search bags for weapons on gang holidays. I learned to be sad that this was a practice that had to happen to keep kids safe. I learned to be grateful that this was the first time I experienced feeling unsafe at school.

I learned compassion and patience. Somehow, I was able to stand up in front of a room full of teenagers and share myself with them and encourage them to open up too. Honestly, I had no idea what I was doing most of the time, but I let the kids lead. I was all in. I was a teacher. I was their teacher and I loved it.

That's how you earn and own a title. You go all in on the path you choose. You may realize on the path that it isn't right, or that you are crawling at times, but if you don't commit, you don't get to say that the path was wrong. You won't learn a thing simply sitting on your life's path. So, go, get in there, look around and offer what you can. Offer the best you can. If you're missing the references here, you didn't listen to your English teacher. Tsk. Tsk. Read

"The Road Not Taken" by Robert Frost. Remember the first two lines: "Two roads diverged in a yellow wood/And sorry I could not travel both." He wrote those lines in 1916. 1916! This is NOT a new conundrum. People have been standing at forks in the road since the beginning of time.

Whatever path you choose to travel, even if it's scary, you are not lost. You made a choice. Even if you look up one day and realize you're not at the right destination, do not panic. Your GPS will reroute you if you made a seriously wrong turn. Welcome your mistakes, thank them, and get ready for the next leg of your adventure. You will surely find your way.

Lesson 5

Objective: Handle a Setback

Teenagers get a bad rap. Seriously, every single time I say I teach high school, I always get the same reaction, "Oh my God! I could never do that."

I get it. Most people think about what they were like in high school. And let's face it, when you look back, just like looking back at your middle school self, it can easily invite an eye roll so dramatic it looks like you are having a stroke. Regardless of your generation, when you look back, your outfit will be questionable, your hairstyle may no longer be working, and you probably will remember many times you were a real jerk to your poor parents because obviously you thought you were smarter than everyone over the age of eighteen. I totally get it. High schoolers can be assholes. It's true. I love them dearly, but high school kids often make questionable decisions.

It's impossible to skip this reckless part of growing up. Sometimes, I wish it wasn't, but these are the unfortunate stories that allow you to make better decisions later on in life. We are products of the excuse, "It was a good idea at the time." Picture classic Tom and Jerry cartoons. You know, when Tom really wants to eat Jerry and then has a brief moment of contemplation. The angel version of himself shows up on his right shoulder and attempts to steer him away from eating poor helpless Jerry. And then, just as Jerry is about to be saved, the devil version of Tom pops up on his left shoulder and convinces him to trust his instinct and enjoy the mouse he's been chasing for eternity. High schoolers often allow the devilish left side to win. It's just the way it is.

You sneak out, you throw parties, you try "things" you were told to "just say no" to, and you sometimes lie to cover up what most adults already know you're doing anyway. Stephanie, who just moved to town decided she would have a few friends over to hang out after school. Of course her mom happily approved. She was relieved to see her daughter joined a team, was keeping her grades up, and was making friends in this new town so quickly. That Friday, the few new friends Stephanie invited quickly turned into a score of friends, as word spread that Stephanie's parents worked over an hour away and would be home late.

Stephanie was feeling uneasy, but like most of you, she was uncomfortable being the buzz kill. This larger-than-expected group were hanging out in Stephanie's basement when one of her new "friends" went out to the garage to grab some ice cream from the freezer. It was there that Stephanie's "friend" spotted a bottle of alcohol and decided to turn Stephanie's "few friends" into a party. Many of the kids who showed up decided to test their limits. It's a classic story. They overdid it. Got drunk, got sick. Regret filled the gaps between the two.

Stephanie and her new "friends" did their best to clean up and aerate the stench of alcohol and puke, but the party smell does not end when the party does. So when Stephanie's parents came home, they took one whiff, looked around, and asked the obvious question, "How many people were here?"

Because Stephanie was in high school, she tried unsuccessfully to lie and was stuck trying to rebuild her parents' trust for the next half of the year. Not to mention, she questioned the new relationships she was trying to foster and had to reevaluate her friend choices before these friendships barely even started. There is a reason why the words *live and learn* are words that live together.

Like I said, no one gets out of adolescence without a few stories worthy of teeth sucking coupled with a head shake and eye roll. Did you ever look back at your old social media posts, videos, tweets, or comments? How about a group text thread that you definitely wouldn't want to reveal outside of the group?

Brittney, an adorable, popular underclassman, realized rather quickly the destruction that could come when words and pictures are left lingering in a digital world. She and her friends were joking and sharing their most recent sexual experiences in a text thread. One of her friends sent an explicit text describing a sexual encounter with her older boyfriend and was asking for advice. Britney chimed in as did the two other girls on the thread.

The responses were supportive, but also revealed the obvious experience of the friend group. Perhaps most of what was written could be deemed typical girl talk, but in a digital world this exchange becomes risky and embarrassing if revealed. A fact many times ignored. You know where this is going, right? Think about the text messages, pictures, apps, and memes that currently exist on your phone, now imagine this:

That evening, Brittney made the mistake of leaving her computer on her desk, unlocked. While she was at volleyball practice, her mom stopped in her room to put Brittney's laundry away and saw the open text thread. While it's easy to be judgmental and angry that Brittney's mom glanced at the computer, saw explicit language, and took the bait, it's also important to be fair that once you create bait, you have to acknowledge that you might catch something.

An extremely awkward conversation ensued when Brittney returned home. It took a long time before she could even look her mom in the eyes, and her mom saw the friends Brittney grew up with through a new, tainted lens. Brittney promptly changed the settings on her text messages and resolved herself to the fact that her relationship with her mom would be strained until they both moved past this unfortunate event.

These moments, these personal setbacks are common. Most of the time, none of these situations, although they result in unfavorable consequences, are meant to be malicious. The culprit is just youth, plain and simple. In fact, most of you will be shocked to discover the outcome of a situation you had no intention of creating.

Real Facts

I used to be baffled by the senior who dug a hole so deep it was going to be near impossible to get him or her to graduation. But now, I see it coming from a mile away. Sometimes, kids sabotage the end of their senior year simply to avoid graduation. Sadly, this is really just a lame attempt to avoid this big scary thing called the real world. The real world, by the way, the one you have already been living in.

Wherever you are and wherever you are headed is real-world stuff. Whoever told you high school wasn't real did you a disservice. I hope you aren't falling for this high school isn't the real-world nonsense.

Cheating on a test in high school matters. You cheat. You show your character. It's real.

Copying your friend's homework and getting credit for pages of equations you have no idea how to solve, matters. You still have no clue how to solve for x. It's real. Filling out college applications and considering spending $40,000 a year or more on a degree that may or may not get you the return on your investment is real. Oh, and the loan you will have to take out and pay back, also real. Even if you're lucky and your parents foot the bill, that is real money too.

The real world is what you are a part of from the day you are born. Good luck trying to convince a preteen who battled cancer, or a child who came from a verbally or physically abusive home that what they endured wasn't real. You don't need to graduate from high school or college to know this: the world can hit you pretty hard at times.

Around the end of May, as my first year of teaching was coming to a close, just before the buzz of June was in the air and the weather started to remind kids to slack off, rumblings of decreased enrollment and budget cuts started to fill the chatter in the teacher's room. A room by the way that is not as glamorous as you may imagine. In fact, let me take a moment to dispel the myth that teachers are in there eating, drinking, and laughing it up between classes. There is no TV, pool table, foosball table, dartboard, or sushi or salad bar.

The teachers' lounge is a room with subpar tables and chairs. It smells mostly like day-old coffee. There is a dirty microwave, and a fridge that isn't cleaned out enough. Both appliances look like they're from a kitchen that existed at least a decade ago. It's a room where teachers eat boring lunches from Lean Cuisine, or last night's leftovers and complain, laugh, and look forward to snow days. That's it. Sorry.

During this time, I had no idea that low student enrollment had anything to do with me. After all, the much older, more experienced people you work with will always talk about stuff you haven't learned yet like 401(k)s, insurance, beneficiaries, longevity, seniority, tax increases, retirement, and the list goes on. So when decreased enrollment popped up, I had no idea that it led to decreased class size, which led to fewer classes, and ultimately fewer teachers.

My principal at the time was a well-respected guy whom everyone was proud to work for. You won't always be lucky enough to feel this way about the people you work for. If you are the one in charge, strive to make your people proud to work for you. It makes a tremendous difference in morale, not to mention everyone will rise to meet the one in charge. When my principal walked the halls, kids scattered. He had an undeniable presence of authority. I don't mean like, *oh hey, there's the guy in charge.* I mean like *here he comes, straighten up and get to class* respected. I mean *don't F-with-the-boss* respected. I mean *kiss-the-ring* respected.

So when my principal called me into his office, it was like, well, getting called to the principal's office minus the long, loud *Ooooooooh* from the rest of the class. I had a bad feeling when I stepped into his office. When I saw his solemn face, I knew I had good reason to feel sick. The room felt heavy and clouded with uncertainty.

The table had a dark, shiny finished wood top and the chairs were leather with a nail head trim; it was a formal, mature space. Sitting there, I felt like a ten-year-old who was caught copying her best friend's math homework in the cafeteria. While he was talking and frowning and delivering the facts, all I could do was try to make sense of the words that seemed to travel through a vacuum of dust and debris: laid off. I sat there and accepted his apologies, regrets, and compliments, followed by *buts* and *howevers*. It was like taking punch after punch and trying to recover between blows. The reality was, I was unemployed again.

Although the tears took a while to form behind the words I struggled to comprehend, I cried. I wanted to be tough and understanding, but, instead, I cried. I cried because the job I loved was gone. I cried because I wasn't a college kid. I cried because my sorority sisters were not my room-mates. I cried because I was a college graduate, and I was in the exact same space I was five years before. The school I loved wasn't mine anymore.

I don't remember exactly how the conversation ended, but I do remember his promises to help me find another job. He said he would make phone calls on my behalf and that he would highly rec-ommend me to any job I wanted. Unfortunately, at that moment, all I could think of was that the job I wanted, he said I couldn't have anymore.

How Do You Cope with Change?

You, too, may find yourself in this unsettling place. This place you had no intention of being in and it can be scary. Okay, it can be terrifying. For the first time, you may find yourself with nowhere to be. No class to rush to, no homework to com-plete, no routine, and no one to answer to. While this may sound like a fantasy when you're in the thick of your high school or college years, it can be unsettling in a time when some of your closest friends are tethered to their dream jobs or enthu-siastically going all in on a start-up. It's inevitable to start comparing your space between with what looks like their solid step forward.

I'm begging you not to do this. It's like Googling chronic head pain when the first two Advil you took after a night of drinking didn't do the trick. Or going on social media after a breakup to stalk your ex. Get it? None of this ends well. It only exacerbates an already unsettling situation. Instead, mind your business. Keep your eyes on your own situation, so you can process what's in front of you.

Disappointment, failure, and embarrassment is not the end of the world. I mean they suck, don't get me wrong, but if you learn to field these emotions, whether it's a dramatic rift with a family member or losing your first job, you get to flex your coping skills. Better still, you will live through these setbacks and see difficult times don't last forever. You will not break. Just like you didn't break from all the questionable decisions you've made, or from the consequences to actions you shouldn't have taken.

You are growing up, and this requires you to be on shaky ground at times. Take a deep breath, try to be rational, and honestly evaluate where you see yourself going as you take the next step that is right for you. That's all you have to do—move thoughtfully forward.

Having confidence in yourself is a lifelong process. And if I am being completely honest with you, which is the point of this entire book, there are still days when I question myself, worry, and feel insecure.

So how do you gain confidence? Through experience. Many, many experiences. There is a reason why the word *gain* is so often connected to confidence. Because it takes time to obtain, much like gaining true friends or, ugh, gaining weight. It doesn't happen overnight. At least it didn't for me. During this time my insecurity was winning. These are the crucial moments you must push through and get to the other side of whatever challenge you are up against. It's like putting a coin in your jar of confidence. Eventually it adds up.

When I stopped in my principal's office and asked for a letter of recommendation, he did what I'll forever be grateful for. He walked me over to his computer, and we wrote that letter together. It was short, to the point, and undeniably stated that he didn't want to let me go. He then suggested that I attach his letter to every résumé I sent out. He thought his letter would fast-track me to the interview. If you can get to the interview, at least you have a shot at landing the job. He was right. A few short months later, I found myself in front of a panel of English teachers. Again.

As you suffer professional setbacks, you will inevitably become a new version of your résumé.

You'll stop pretending to be all the fabulous points you carefully added on your résumé, and you will stop trying to convince people that you can do the job you're not even sure you want. Believe me, you will be far from perfect, but you will begin to speak from a place that exudes excitement and passion, because your experience will start to solidify who you really are, and you will start to see clearly where you want to go. This is the gift that is left behind after you suffer a hit.

I learned later being on the other side of the interview table that these qualities were better than any binder full of sample projects, high test scores, and a fancy college degree. Tara, you know my friend who obtained that health science degree, went on to get her master's degree in human resources and now hires and fires people on a regular basis for a global corporation. She always looks for candidates who seem to fit with the culture and values of the team. The education line and all those fancy bullets that sparkle with your qualifications on a résumé will only shine if you can back them up and play nice with others.

Remember this as you move forward. You are better than what your résumé says, just like you are probably better than that college application you sent out. Pull it together, stand on top of the

lessons you've learned through experiences you
didn't expect, and believe in who you have become.
Get ready to show what you have to offer as a professional and as a person.

You are better than whatever throws you off
balance personally or professionally. You have to
be okay because the alternative is giving up. If you
have come this far, you are not a quitter. If you are
reading these words, you care about getting better and have a level of awareness that you probably
don't give yourself credit for.

Even when you are thrown off balance like a
chunky kid on a seesaw, push yourself up. It won't
be the last time you hit the ground. But you won't
stay there. There will always be ups and downs.
So when you find yourself unexpectedly suffering from the after-effects of an earthquake, let the
dust settle, evaluate what needs to be cleaned up,
and get moving.

Objective: Move On

My sister-in-law works for a major bottling company. She works so hard, we often joke that she owns the company and is just keeping it a secret from the rest of us so we won't sponge off her millions. She has worked at the same company for decades and has outlasted even some of the people she has worked for. She is well-liked at her job and is often invited to company outings and events, most of which she plans.

Nevertheless when she is required to attend meetings with some big players in the room, she stresses. When she chimes in during meetings, or when it's her turn to report back to the group, she worries how her comments will be received. I bet this same scenario has played out for you countless times.

It's kind of like when you raise your hand in class. You ask or answer a question and then repeat it in your head to make sure it sounded okay. How about when you start to make a comment or give an example and you can't stop talking, and before you know it, you catch yourself in a full-on ramble. When you finally stop talking is when the overthinking kicks in. *Did that make sense? What was I trying to say? I hope that didn't sound stupid. I wish I didn't raise my hand. I sure hope I didn't offend anyone.*

It's normal to overthink or get stuck when you care, but it's also a total waste of time. Just so you know, no one in the meeting or in class spent any time perseverating over your comments like you did. Oh, don't get me wrong, I'm sure you're a big deal, but I've learned everyone is mostly too busy worrying about themselves to expend energy on comments, unless they have a direct effect. So why is it so hard to find security in the fact that you did your best and let the rest go?

I don't care who you are. Most of us get stuck worrying about what people think or what we might be missing out on because of our need to have solid connections, whether they are at work or in private. Don't worry. It's not just you, it's human nature. No one has hopes and dreams of having no friends, no partner, no job, or wakes up and thinks, *My life would be perfect, if only I was a lone loser.*

Quite frankly, rejection sucks. Our desire to be accepted by people or places that we value make it especially hard to move past when we find ourselves in a rut. How about when you can't have something or someone and then you want it, him, or her even more? This fixation on what isn't for you can be like quicksand and only gets tougher and tougher to get out of the longer you allow yourself to linger in the thick sludge of the situation you find yourself in.

Don't Get Stuck

Good news. There is actually a way to get out of quicksand. Obviously, your initial reaction will be to start struggling and, unless you are Indiana Jones, you will probably panic. It's proven, however, that you can free yourself from quicksand by first relaxing and letting go of whatever weight you are carrying that isn't necessary. Then you can slowly start to free yourself by using small methodical movements to pull your legs to a horizontal position while also leaning back. The goal is to then swim toward safety. All of this becomes much easier if you have access to a walking stick or someone with you to give you a helping hand to push yourself out of the struggle.

Stop with the furrowed brow. I know I can't prove this method. I'm a New Yorker who doesn't even drive off-road, but Google and my seven-year-old says this is proven. It's also documented that being in quicksand itself will not kill you. However, it's probably a good idea to avoid quicksand if you can.

In other words, don't get stuck holding onto thoughts, people, or places that do not serve your next move or make you feel less than. Dump the negative beliefs like an overstuffed backpack that is making you heavy and ultimately helping you sink faster. You don't need to struggle or panic. You are not going to die. Moving on can start with the smallest of steps. Falling forward is still forward and helpful. So, move. Ready or not. I hope it is also not lost on you that helping hands should be held onto if you see one. Grab it. There is no room for your ego in quicksand.

It was summertime—one of those days when the heat has you sweating like a kid waiting in line to ride a way-too-big, way-too-scary roller coaster, listening to people scream as they descend each loop. There was no turning back. Black pencil skirt and a white cotton, button-down collared shirt. Same black bag. This time it was filled with a portfolio of lesson plans and actual work from students I actually taught. Low, modest, black heels. Thank goodness my purple suit had long before found its way to Goodwill. Side note: You should get rid of bad outfits too.

They called my name, and just as I suspected, a panel of English teachers sat, like Knights of the Round Table, ready to open fire and shoot me with questions. Isn't it great when you realize you're living a moment that can change everything? Makes you want to jump for joy and run like your hair is on fire all at the same time. Either way, it's your move.

The people around the table were most likely teaching when I was learning to read. Well, except for one girl who looked about my age and less intimidating. She looked like we could have easily been friends in high school or college. The rest of them looked like, well, English teachers: buttoned up and ready to correct my grammar.

There were two other women besides my friendly peer. One introduced herself as the head of the department, and the other introduced herself as the principal. They both greeted me with what felt like mom smiles. You know the mom smile, it's the one when your mom smiles, but with her eyes she is saying, "I'm watching you, so watch your step."

There were two men at the table too. One looked like he could've played Sherlock Holmes in one of the mysteries my grandma watches on TV, and the other looked like Conan O'Brien without the friendly smile and sense of humor. These five people held the next big move of my life in their hands. Or so I thought. I took a deep breath and did what I learned to do in interviews: use confidence to hide fear.

I thanked them all as the interview came to a close and left feeling confident that I would get the chance to see them all again. This is one of the benefits of being forced to try something you didn't expect, or forced to try something different: you get the chance to trust in your abilities. You see, when you decide to make a move, any move, you are actually the one in control. It is your decision or series of decisions that lands you in the opportunities that can alter your world. So while it might feel like people in big, important rooms hold your fate in their hands, it's actually up to you to take control, rise up to the room, and get out of your head.

The call from the principal came a few days later, and I was invited to meet with the district's assistant superintendent. She reviewed the district's mission and then opened a copy of the current contract between the school district and the teachers' union. She ran her finger down the page and then across a line of numbers until she landed on the offered salary based on my education, at the time I had a BA, and my one year of teaching experience. I squinted to make sure I was seeing the numbers correctly because this spot in the contract made my previous pay look subpar. It also had me wondering why I didn't get the leather interior in my new car. Damn it.

I went from a college graduate to unemployed, to a first-year teacher, to unemployed, back to a first-year teacher in a different school district. Just like that.

Ali, the sweet young girl who sat across from me asking questions during the interview, volunteered to be my mentor. We were colleagues, and more than that, we became fast friends. I don't mean we sat in the teachers' room and ate lunch together, although we often did that too. I mean we actually became friends. Ali had recently broken off an engagement, and my college boyfriend and I had recently broken up, too, so we quickly bonded over lost love and found ourselves going out, being single, and having fun. It was a friendship that showed up at exactly the right time. Most great friendships often do.

Another perk of getting up and moving forward: new people often show up. Think back to the moves you've already made in your life. Who popped up that made that move worth it? Your lab partner in the AP class you decided to take, the kid who was put on your peewee football team, the new girl who walked into your SAT prep course, the fraternity brothers you inherited upon initiation, the clients who gave you five-star reviews, and the countless other people who became present in your world because you made a choice.

My new colleague became one of my best friends. I later found out that after my interview, our department leader mentioned how great I would be for Ali. She imagined us working together, learning from each other, and becoming seasoned English teachers together. This is exactly how our friendship unfolded. I hope you find these people in your life too. In high school, college, at work, or wherever you find yourself doing your thing.

Because these connections make *doing your thing* into a life worth living.

Three short months ago I had been crying in my principal's office over a job I loved and lost. Somehow I managed to push myself back into the running for other opportunities and struck teaching gold. My assignment was a perfect fit for me. I was asked to teach tenth-grade English, and they offered me the opportunity to design a course titled Mass Media.

How do you get here? You have to be willing to be the new guy or the new girl, again.

I threw on my teacher clothes, by this time I had many outfits that fit the bill, and alas the bell rang. That year, I met over a hundred new students, and I met colleagues who helped shape me as a teacher and challenged me as a person. I can't imagine who I would be if I was never let go from my first job. A job I would have never left on my own.

I often tell my students this story. The story of how I wound up standing in front of them. The story of how I didn't want to leave my first teaching job, but working with them was a blessing then and is still a blessing every day. Yes, even days when they cheat, or vape, or mumble profanities when I hand back bleeding essays. When I stand before them, I see that they do not see the golden ticket that is their education. I try desperately to look back and remember, but I'm sure I didn't understand the value of my education in high school either.

You're probably in the same boat too. As much as I want to shake them, I can't blame them or you. Between classes, sports, relationships, family pressure, and college apps hovering, any hallelujah in gratitude for education will have to wait. Just know, one of the best moves you can make is to live in a mindset that education, a commitment to being a lifelong learner, will serve you well.

High school is exciting, overwhelming, challenging, lonely, boring, interesting, frustrating, and filled with possibility all at the same time. It's a time when you are still under your parents' thumbs; teachers assess whether you are worthy of a passing grade; and yet you are expected to make big moves, grand decisions, and grow up. Don't you dare chug a beer, though, you're not twenty-one!

Most teachers will even require you to ask permission to use the bathroom. Not this teacher, but most also like you to sit in an assigned seat. It's a random time between being a kid and being an adult. It's tough at some point for all of us. The uncertainty and doubt is palpable. Luckily, high school is a place you don't get to hold onto; quite frankly, there are few places we get to keep. It's four fast years that kick you out into your next big move.

While you're in high school, you'll be asked a million times: What are you doing after high school? This is of course attached to another loaded question:

What Do You Want to Be When You Grow Up?

It's always a fun question to ask elementary school kids. Currently, my ten-year-old wants to be a star in the NFL, and a part-time magician. I remember my nephew Sal declaring, "I want to be the Incredible Hulk!" As he got older, he learned this wouldn't work. Perhaps it was around the same year he discovered being Buzz Lightyear for Halloween didn't actually mean he could fly. Like all of us who grow and change our goals, he reassessed.

As years passed, and Sal changed, so did his answer to the question: What do you want to be when you grow up? He declared, "I want to be a New York Yankee." And then he discovered lacrosse.

The point is, as children, the answer to this question is exciting. The possibilities are endless, and most of us answer without fear. Hell. We declare it.

My niece wants to be an eye doctor. My three-year-old wants to be a dinosaur. No ifs, ands, or buts about it. How's that for an endless possibility?

I have a senior in my class who wants nothing more than to be a contestant on *Survivor.* She fearlessly submits an application every time a casting call is announced. While most of us watch this type of show for entertainment, she watches and thinks, "I can do that." This is the type of conviction I wish I could give to every single one of you as you move on from a place of uncertainty, to solid ground, to uncertainty, to solid ground, and on, and on, and on.

I told my parents I would be a writer when I was in elementary school. Okay. Bad example. Later, as a freshman in high school, being a Knicks City Dancer swirled around my brain. I was a member of my high school's dance company, so this made perfect sense at the time. I wish I could insert my favorite eye roll emoji here coupled with the dark-haired girl with the purple shirt whose palm is on her forehead in a constant state of horror; this admission is cringe worthy. Because now, I get down in Zumba class and when I catch a glimpse of myself in the mirror, I am shocked to see I do not look like I belong in a viral TikTok dance video. It's a good thing I moved on.

Seriously, read this next part carefully. Even when you grow up and you choose, the question still applies: What do you want to be? Because like your elementary school self, your high school self, and your adult self, you will shift, grow, and change an endless amount of times during your life. Sometimes, like for me early on in my career, you are forced to change even when you don't want to.

You may want nothing more than to plant your flag on that first college that accepts you, or that first job that hires you, or put all your energy into the first idea you have on your way to entrepreneurship. It might be tempting to stay in what becomes a new comfort zone. But, trust me, holding on with white knuckles to a career path that is pushing you away doesn't work.

This goes for friends and relationships too. Imagine if you never opened up your friend group, or never let go of friends that you grew out of. Many times, if you just let go and allow the shifts to happen and allow yourself to move with the change, you will easily find happiness in this uncharted territory.

I am a teacher. I know who I am now. Standing up in front of a bunch of teenagers reading J. D. Salinger's final scene in *The Catcher in the Rye* is my Super Bowl. Holden realizes that his younger sister will grow up and fail and get back up count-less times while reaching for success. He can't stop it; he can't protect her. He has to let her go, and he needs to move on too. Holden gets a bad rap; he lands on the banned books list all the time. Most likely because he reveals a truth we are all so uncomfortable with. Sooner or later, we all must grow up, and growing up can be hard.

Today, you may be a student, an athlete, an intern, a podcaster, a YouTube Star, or a DoorDash driver. Tomorrow, you could start a blog, or decide to hop a plane to Europe. Who knows? The point is the answer changes and you will too. We all do.

So go ahead, grow up and keep growing. Get a job, get laid off, get promoted, transfer depart-ments, pursue a degree, apply for a new job, start a business, move to a new city, whatever it may be, keep evolving. You will fail. You will be let go. You may be pushed, but you will survive whatever quicksand you stumble into. There is no need to panic, but don't just stand there or you'll sink. Keep your people close, and ask for support when you need it. Pressing pause is not an option, so get used to looking forward and make your moves count.

Objective: Be Brave

How many teenagers have I been blessed to meet? The math goes roughly like this: Five classes a day with twenty to twenty-eight kids in each class, times two for semester classes, times twenty-ish years. You do the math. No, seriously, you do the math. I'm your English teacher.

Sure. I did what I had to do to get myself through college algebra, but I'm not about to solve an equation here in my book. So I don't know the exact answer to that equation. But here's what I do know: I know teenagers. And because of this fact, I am confident to tell you with unwavering faith that you—yes, you—are braver than you think. And because of this simple fact, you must learn to trust yourself.

While we spend many years, typically from middle school through high school, trying to figure out who we are, we also spend most of our days being told what to do and who to do what with. This is all happening while we fight desperately for our independence. Your family may even sit you at the kids table at Thanksgiving and then on the ride home ask you how you fielded questions about the college process.

Seriously, this time in our lives makes no sense. Not sure if you're ready for that R-rated movie, but what do you want to do with the rest of your life? Get a job. Your job is getting in the way of your schoolwork. Please pick up your little brother from practice. You're never home. How in the world are you supposed to get it right with all these mixed messages?

It's a cruel joke the universe plays on all of us. Basically, this quagmire is not new. I repeat: this is not new. You should feel comfort in this simple fact. We are all essentially cut from the same cloth, even your parents went through it. It's called adolescence, the coming of age, growing up, finding yourself, the shit show, or whatever catch phrase you choose. And, many times, most times, it's not pretty.

Actually, it's pretty awful at times. I mean, have you seen a middle school yearbook lately? Have you checked out your own middle school yearbook lately? It's brutal: the hair, the braces, the awkward proportion between that which grew and that which did not grow, yet. It's rough. But if you scan each square on the page, you'll see the faces of kids all in the same boat. That boat is the *SS Adolescence,* and, many times, each of those passengers may feel stuck as if they were on board the *Titanic.* Only there is no iceberg, so this boat sails on to high school.

As it sails, as it rides the waves, the passengers keep showing up. And you are tossed around this moving ship desperately searching for something to cling to, anything to keep you on solid ground. The good news is that you, my friend, are still standing because you are brave. I know this because I have lived in the presence of teenagers.

Through my students, I have learned to take off my life vest and to be vulnerable. This has made all the difference in my life. Students are behind every word in this book. Words that I may have never written if they did not model courage. While my job is to believe in them, they believe in me too. And while my job is to teach, many times, I am the one being taught.

Here are just a few things I have learned: Tests go beyond the page and homework can be hard for those without a home or support from home. I learned the bad kids aren't bad, they are hurt. I learned that students are kids and kids are people and all people need love. When the bell rings, class isn't over.

Countless students have lingered after the bell. Sometimes it's just to ask a question about the day's lesson, but most often it's to talk, share some news, or express a concern. I hear *Ugh! I have a test today, I'm so tired, I have so much work to do, I hate everybody, I wish it was Friday, and I'm starving.* a million times a week. Sometimes, students milling around after the bell aren't even sure why. But they are waiting for me. It took me a long time to figure this out; sometimes they need me to simply ask, "What's going on?"

Over the years it has surprised me that kids will easily open up with this simple prompt. The usual response is, "Ah, nothing." But any follow-up question typically opens the flood gate of prom drama, worries about college, a fight with a friend, or an angry text from mom.

Just today, the bell rang, and one of my sophomores quietly stood in front of my desk and politely asked, "What do you think happened to

Holden Caulfield after he left the institution?"
Now, clearly, I have no idea what the actual
answer to this question is because, well, Salinger
never wrote a follow-up book to *The Catcher in the
Rye*, and he certainly wasn't the type of author to
sit around and discuss his books with the media.
Oh, and also, he's dead.

I knew immediately that this question had
little to do with concern for Holden Caulfield's
well-being and everything to do with something
my student had weighing her down. I told her
that I hoped if Salinger wrote another chapter to
The Catcher in the Rye, it would reveal that Holden
learned to communicate with his family and rely
on them for support. I told her I would have loved
to see Holden go back to school and use his critical
mind. I then said, "Why? What's going on? Why
are you thinking about Holden?"

And then came her tears. She revealed an issue
she was having with her friends and how she didn't
know how to handle one friend who was making
poor choices. She told me she tried to talk to her parents about it, but they dismissed her worries as high
school drama and no big deal. I listened and vali-
dated: it *is* a big deal. It may not matter tomorrow,
or next week, and it most definitely won't matter in
a year, but in high school, sometimes, this drama

almost becomes too much to bear. And this drama happens every day. To be honest, she didn't reveal anything I haven't heard a million times before.

This never gets old for me. This is probably my favorite part of my job. I love being one of the adults they trust. While I spend most of my day discussing how to prove a controversial thesis statement, and explaining why Shakespeare is still magical in our modern time (don't roll your eyes at me), I am fairly sure, no, I'm positive that these conversations trump content every time.

This has also been the hardest part of my job. My heart has broken so many times for my brave students who have revealed difficulties in their lives and trusted me to hold their stories with compassion. Some of the bravest students I've ever met emerged on a peer leadership retreat where several teachers spent two days team building and bonding with students. The purpose of this trip is to learn strategies for problem solving and communication to better serve the incoming freshman class. This retreat is also the perfect time to prove to students that because we are all human, we have a common bond. Through this simple fact we can relate to each other even if we first appear to be complete opposites.

Altering a page from Rachel Hollis's book, spe-cifically her RISE conference activity called *Stand Up for Your Sister,* students engaged in a similar activity called *Stand Up for Your Peer.* Over fifty teenagers sat in a large circle and were given pens and paper. They were asked to check all the boxes that applied to their experiences.

At first, they were hesitant to start making checkmarks. I watched them slowly read down the list they were given. Many of them looked up and around before beginning to mark their pages. I noticed several kids making sure their responses couldn't be seen. The paper contained the follow-ing statements:

☐ I have lived through my parents' divorce.

☐ I have had my heart broken.

☐ I have felt ugly.

☐ I have felt like a loser.

☐ I have failed a test, project, essay, or class.

☐ I didn't make the team.

☐ I have endured being mistreated—emotionally, physically, verbally, digitally.

☐ I have suffered from stress, depression, anxiety, or panic.

☐ I have lost someone close to me.

☐ I have worried about my future.

This was completed anonymously, and then students were told to fold pages into small rectangles. Then the folded pages were rotated around the room and traded across the circle until it was impossible to know who marked which page. When each participant had another's paper, he or she was to reveal which boxes were checked by standing up.

One by one the statements were read aloud. As each statement was read, students were to stand up from their chairs if they held a paper with that statement checked. We all sadly looked around. I paused between sentences to catch my breath and process the pain hanging in this microcosm of the world. The emotional weight in the room was thick and heavy, but everyone in that space held it together.

"I have felt like a loser" filled the circle as every student stood up.

Have you ever felt this way? Look back at the list. How many of these statements apply to you? If you are human, I would imagine this list looks familiar. It sure does for most of the teenagers I know. Truth be told, most of this list applied to my high school self too.

I know there is no way to prevent you from this inevitable adolescent self-doubt. My heart swelled with love for these kids and my fifteen-year-old self. We all prevailed at that moment. A moment of vulnerability that helped to strengthen students so they may lead and guide others that may be lost. The heart of these actions is pure courage. I watched students look around the room and realize, to their surprise, they were not alone in the hardships of high school. I urge you to look around too. I bet you are among silent friends who understand more than you know.

This I Believe

This is one of countless times I have seen a student rise to a challenge and move an entire room. I have learned that sometimes, many times, the curriculum is unimportant if it is so overwhelming that students get lost in the weeds.

When I first started teaching, I stayed the course. If content was on the curriculum, I got it done. I never missed a book, an essay, not even a short story or poem missed its turn in my lesson plans. I thought being a good teacher meant teaching it all. Rushing through the day's lesson if that's what it took. But as I learned to meet kids where they needed me, I learned to take my foot off the gas and look around.

As a result of a recommendation from my teaching colleague, I made time for an assignment called *This I Believe*. An assignment that proved to be so valuable it quickly became a standard part of the curriculum. The assignment has a long history dating back to the 1950s. It was first made famous by a radio host and then was reignited in 2009 by NPR. The idea behind it is for people to declare one belief they hold dear. Then writers must prove their personal belief based on actual experiences.

Ask any adult to do this and you may get a great paper, but can they get up in front of a room of their peers and read it raw? Well, my students can. I challenge you to complete this same assignment too; you'll be amazed to see what emerges.

"I believe with good comes bad," one student wrote. The paper, essentially the monologue, delivered in class proceeded to reveal a past where cutting proved to be the only way to feel in a time of deep depression. A time that a young girl not only lived to tell about, but also learned about herself, her issues, and the importance of reaching out for help. She stood up before her classmates and without abandon read her story.

She stopped only once to gather herself. She apologized politely for the break in her story and swallowed tears. The room was still and respectful. She finished strong and her peers nodded and clapped as they held her in a safe space. And just like that she showed strength in the wake of sharing how emotionally fragile she once felt.

"Thank you for sharing," I whispered.

It always amazes me when kids put themselves out in front of their peers and reveal something magical about themselves. Never forget, it takes one voice to close the gap between people.

Another student, who had been missing from class for four days came back to school and volunteered to read her essay to me and the room packed with her classmates. I was pleased to see she had been following along with the online lessons and worked to complete the posted assignment. She seemed eager to share and I was surprised to hear this:

I believe in mental health . . . Imagine this: you wake up on a Wednesday morning with this inexplicable feeling of dread overtaking you. You're exhausted . . . Getting up and out of bed is a physical pain for you, and you can barely keep your eyes open as you force yourself out the door and off to school. Now, imagine going into school and sitting in your classes, staring at the work before you and finding yourself unable to register a word of what you are reading. You heard the instruction the teacher gave to the class, so you know what you're supposed to be doing. However, your mind is shutting down. The drive to complete your assignments that you'd normally have seems to have vanished. In this state, you aren't even mentally present enough to even begin to do one simple assignment. This has happened to me.

As this brave student finished reading her essay, and revealed her absences from class were due to her ongoing battle with depression, not the more widely accepted excuse of a physical ailment, I turned to the class and asked, "How many of you have ever felt like you couldn't get out of bed? Or like facing the day ahead was a struggle?" Every hand went up including mine. The whole room seemed to exhale.

Once again, one stands up and many show you're never alone. Don't be afraid to be the one.

Are You Proud of Yourself?

I learned that when students are challenged, they rise. I wish teenagers knew how often they win. I hope you note the wins in your life and give yourself room to acknowledge small victories and step up when you know you can.

High school for so many is a time where troubles seem to stand out and stick out far more than the fun and triumph. I urge you to see it clearly. See the reality of how far you've come even if there are some dark spots, continue to look for growth. Some of my students see it and I hope you can too.

If you think reading books like *The Old Man and the Sea*, *Wuthering Heights*, *Our Town (Oof!)*, and anything written by Shakespeare were boring in high school, you should try reading them two to three times a day for twenty years. I probably shouldn't admit this, but we've come this far and there really is no turning back. You might as well know: sometimes your teachers get bored too. Therefore, as you can imagine, to stay sane, variety in delivery is essential.

Teaching public speaking is no different. Don't get me wrong, I love teaching kids to public speak. It's always fun to watch kids come in on the first day and reveal they got stuck in my class because it was the only class that fit their schedules. These are usually the kids that make the greatest strides over the course of the semester because they are so painfully shy at the start. Up is the only way they can go.

I also love the three major speeches I teach because I know my students will be faced with delivering demonstration, informative, and persuasive speeches in college. But how many times can I watch kids do a demo on how to make guacamole, or a persuasive speech on lowering the drinking age? Not to mention I teach this course sometimes three times a year. Needless to say, I was searching for a curve ball to throw at kids that selfishly might also be refreshing for me.

At the time, I just started to listen to podcasts and stumbled upon *The Ed Mylett Show* (a podcast). I also just finished reading books by Ed Mylett, Rachel Hollis, and Gabrielle Bernstein. I could indulge in this kind of content all day long. I started to analyze their motivational speaking techniques and I thought, *hey I should try this with my kids.*

After watching a bunch of videos and picking up the different approaches used by speakers, I delivered a motivational speech to get kids fired up about planning and delivering their own motivational speeches. It was so different, and fun. The kids loved it, too, and many of them volunteered to give it a try. I really didn't know what I was going to get, but sometimes the universe puts the right twenty to twenty-eight kids in the same room, and magic happens.

One student got up in front of the class and told his story of triumph over his learning disability. It began with a teacher's painful words. She warned his mom in front of his impressionable ears, "School just isn't for everyone." And the final blow, he was "too difficult" for her to manage in class. These hurtful words stuck with him for his entire educational career.

But as a brave high school senior, he stood up in front of our class, swallowed tears, and expressed how this pain fueled his work ethic and helped him grow and mature as a learner. The story ended with a heartfelt moment that revealed his acceptance to the college of his dreams. A college that not only accepted him, but issued him an academic scholarship to guarantee his attendance in the fall.

Students clapped at the story laced with pain and success and understood its motivational plea to never let anyone tell you what you can and cannot accomplish. That semester, he was one of many brave students who told stories tangled with tough stuff that ended with inspiring lessons that helped shape their growth and closed the gap in the audience.

One student in that class slated to pursue teaching, decided to abandon what she always thought she would do, and is now pursuing a career as a life coach and motivational speaker. She launched her own podcast shortly after delivering a twenty-two-minute speech to her peers on pursuing your life's passion. She spoke from her heart, grabbed an audience full of her peers, and held onto their heartstrings.

She came to me after class and blurted out, "I can't believe I just did that!" That same student went on to deliver a motivational speech to a packed auditorium as part of her final senior project. As she thanked the audience for coming, teachers and students were on their feet celebrating her unbelievable ability to move an audience.

Imagine this same public speaking classroom a few years earlier, welcoming a student from the Dominican Republic who spoke not one word of English. Can you stand up in front of a room of twenty-five people and deliver a five- to seven-minute speech after a few short weeks living in a foreign country? This student who, by simply getting up in front of my room and trying, taught our entire class that year to try and fail and try and fail until you come out on the other side of a challenge stronger than when you started.

These snapshots of kids killing it and teaching each other how to be brave are only a few of the many moments teenagers have shined in my room and in their world. I learned that once a student graduates, he or she is still my student. I will always be Ms. Curcio or Mrs. Pyrch to the countless kids who walked in and out of my room. Because that's where your teacher stays. In that classroom that you remember, teaching lessons that you will forget, pushing you out of your comfort zone and encouraging you to try. Those adults that worry, complain, and criticize "kids today," have nothing to worry about. These kids today have a lot to teach us. You have a lot to teach us.

Your stories matter. Your stories—made up of moments where you pushed yourself to do something you thought you couldn't do—will be all you remember about high school, so go big and know you can because you are brave.

Objective: Get Your Heart Broken

hen does the word *falling* precede a positive experience? Think about it: falling on your face, falling down the stairs, falling over the couch, falling out of the car, falling off the chair, falling in a hole, falling under the table. None of these falls are typically favorable, yet most of us ooh and ahh at the idea of falling in love. Falling, by its very nature, leaves you in a vulnerable place, alone, waiting to make contact with something, often unexpected. The sheer possibility that you can fall into another person's world, find love, and make magic is why, no matter how many times falling in love leads you to missing your mark, most of us continue to jump. Only a few of us get it right the first time, which is why hearts break—yet have the ability to heal.

There is no secret sauce for avoiding the pain of heartbreak. I wish there were, because I would serve that shit on a daily basis to every kid who has come to class upset or cut class because of the total devastation of a broken heart. *Who didn't get asked to the prom, who said yes, then backed out, who kissed who at the party, and who posted what on social media?* Broken hearts do not discriminate. Boys have cried in my room, girls have cried in my room, and I have cried in my room. Yes, your teacher has experienced heartbreak too.

Unfortunately, you may have experienced your first heartbreak through watching your parents struggle to sustain a marriage in a stressful house filled with the overwhelm of daily responsibilities. You may have witnessed fights you shouldn't have heard about topics you didn't understand. Nevertheless, without your consent, you began to develop ideas about relationships and how they work. This is never the intention of parents, unless of course you grew up with parents who lived a storybook romance, always maintained respectful communication, and never fought. Highly doubtful.

Either way, your upbringing has an influence, whether you like it or not, and many times it will inform your choices in relationships and impact the person you choose to love.

Witnessing the pain, disappointment, and often anger associated with a marriage that isn't working or that ends in divorce can leave you heartbroken. The raw deal is that you didn't even get to experience the rush of falling in love. You just got told that you get to continue to love two hearts who fell out of love whether they choose to live together or not. You see, no one oohs and ahhs at this part, but this part is real and hurts like hell.

The number of college essays I've read by writers who attempt to find forgiveness, peace, and hope in the wake of this heartbreak are countless. Some even find gratitude and reap the benefits of knowing that new love can emerge from the pain left when love does not prevail. Many have lived through loss, transient pseudo-parental figures, and were forced to grow up too fast as they uncovered flaws in their parents they weren't ready to see.

Regardless of the heartbreak you witnessed or felt during your childhood, you will instinctively continue to search for love for yourself. This includes those of you who swear you'll never get married and spend many years creating a well-built wall around your heart too. Love is a universal need, so the same way you search for snacks when your body registers hunger, so will you be drawn to love.

And, on that search, like on most quests, you will run into the rise and fall of your love story. Both the ups and downs are uncertain, but the possibility of finding what great love stories are made of is enough for most of us to blow around untethered with unwavering hope that love will find us.

Tim O'Brien, in his book *The Things They Carried,* wrote that stories can save us. Stories of heartbreak are not easy to write and put under a microscope, so forgive me while I squirm in my seat and forget that you are actually reading this. I wouldn't exactly pick this time of my life to relive, but it is this space that eventually served me well and taught me to love the right way.

You might be in the middle of a messy love story too. You see, heartbreak is a harsh teacher who shows up, reminds you to love yourself first, and knows you can do better. Heartbreak is relentless and will keep showing up until you find the right love.

Warning: What you are about to read here is the best version of my truth. Here's the thing:

When the heart breaks, there are two sides to the broken heart. And, in most cases, it doesn't break into two equal parts. Therefore, the two sides of this broken heart story, like most of yours, probably don't match.

Monday Morning Quarterback

After a year of teaching at my new second job, I was asked by a few of my students to coach the cheerleading team. *Cheerleading?* I thought. I only cheered for basketball one season in high school, and I do not remember bringing anything on, if you know what I mean. But I was not going to say no to an extra stipend and a chance to be the head cheerleader in high school. I mean, the coach of the team.

I inherited a list of ancient cheers, and at twenty-four years old, I became a cheerleader. V-I-C-T-O-R-Y! I was not this girl in high school. So as an adult, with an undergrad degree, retired Greek letters, many friends, a job, and now a cheerleading sweatshirt that said *Coach*, I fell in love with this new persona. Falling in love often comes with a few shots of confidence too. It felt like high school, only this time I wasn't in the stands immortalizing the upperclassmen hoping to land at the right party after the game. I didn't long for a varsity jersey with a senior football player's name on it. I was an adult. I thought I was above the adolescent insecurity and desire to date above my social status, but old habits die hard.

As this heartbreak story begins, the assistant coach of our football team (we will call him Tommy) was also my age, and because we were basically in high school, it didn't take long before we noticed each other on the sidelines. I didn't even consider the warnings about dating in the workplace. This was the quarterback of the football team. I mean the assistant coach. I wasn't going to pass up any attention he had to offer. I couldn't help it; I was drawn to the wrapping paper before I even knew what was inside.

This relationship had all the makings of a great high school drama. It was as good as *Saved by the Bell, Beverly Hills 90210, Dawson's Creek, One Tree Hill*, and, of course, *Friday Night Lights*. At twenty-four I was riding high. Tommy pursued me with abandon. He went from going out of his way to talk to me on the sidelines, to meeting up with me after work, to spending every night with me. For the first time in my life, I didn't hold back either. I was so in love with the story around our relationship that I jumped in headfirst without using my head.

Consider the people and things that you are drawn to and pull at your heart. These choices can stem from your past, your long-term goals, or some fantasy you are chasing. Who or what do you long for? *If only I had—* When you fill in the blank does it contribute to who you truly aspire to be, does it align with your core values, or does it feed into a facade you are trying to create? Make sure you know the difference, because youth can make you reckless when it comes to matters of the heart, and love is a rule breaker.

In high school, most of you are so exhausted from the pressure and workload that it's easy to lose sight of who you really are and align yourself with people who appear safe or keep you in good social standing. Time to reflect when days are rushing by can be difficult to come by. But doing self-checks on your choices and the people you surround yourself with is key to developing into the best version of yourself, instead of into some superficial version who exists to gain approval from people who probably won't matter beyond graduation day.

High school can be tough on your sense of self. So, sure, I was a cool teacher, but I was nothing like her in high school. He, on the other hand, was the quarterback of his high school football team.

In other words, he was high school royalty. Early on he even said to me, "You know, I could choose anyone here, but I chose you." I latched onto this statement and held onto it like a first place trophy.

If I'm writing the truth, and believe me I am trying to, just so you don't feel so alone, this fact made the love exciting and why I held onto it for so long. It felt like validation for all those years in high school when I was passed over for a more popular girl even though my intentions were pure and my heart was open.

Embarrassing, right? The truth is, it's easy to weigh in on a relationship that you are not in. *What's she doing with him? Oh my goodness, she walks all over him. Doesn't he see she's just using him? He cheats on her all the time, I feel so bad for her. Everyone knows she lies to him.* I'm sure this all sounds familiar.

Because, when you're not in it, from the outside looking in, it's easy to judge troubled relationships. Then suddenly as you become the one in love, it's like you had too many drinks, the music is too loud, and everything starts to become a little fuzzy. Love coupled with youth is like a shot of Fireball with a chaser. This is why Shakespeare wrote, "Love is blind," and this truth will never die.

Tommy liked to have a little too much fun. I don't mean the frat boy behavior that was all in good fun. I mean the antics that ended in tears, or an argument. At the time, I was too afraid to lose him to admit how uncomfortable I was with it. I learned to laugh it off, to deflect from the pain I often felt in front of people who loved me and wanted me to be happy. I allowed myself to believe that he wasn't being disrespectful when he flirted with other girls. I told myself that he was just a friendly guy and I had nothing to worry about because I won: he chose me. I convinced myself that when we were alone, he was perfect and that was enough. I learned the hard way that it wasn't. He wasn't. The relationship wasn't.

Take a Knee

When you lose in love, it's easy to point fingers. The people who love you will probably say things like, "He didn't deserve you," or "Her loss," or the old "I never liked him." While this may very well all be true, what good is it? His fault, her fault, your fault all become irrelevant when you are sitting by yourself on a Friday night watching *The Notebook* feeling sorry for yourself. You know what does help? Figuring out what mistakes you made that contributed to the breakup and being mindful that you won't repeat them. This part isn't fun. But if you play the victim card without looking at the other cards in your hand, you have little chance of ever winning.

Tommy's career in physical fitness and unpredictable income was not going to work for my "go to college, get a job, support yourself" upbringing, so I tried to make Tommy a version of himself that would allow me to live comfortably with him. The problem was, I don't think I actually ever asked Tommy if he wanted a solution to a problem he didn't know he had. I just decided he should go back to school and get a degree in education.

Tommy was pursuing a career he didn't choose, and I was so busy pressing the gas on our future that I refused to admit that the relationship was falling apart. I knew it, but I was not brave enough or willing to let go. I had written our story and I was determined to live it: *The cheer coach and the football coach live happily ever after.* I held on no matter what. I am talking white-knuckled held on. Exactly what I told you not to do in the last chapter because it never works. Didn't work with my first job, and it certainly didn't work with this relationship.

You know this relationship; you might have even lived this relationship. These are the romantic movie archetypes we swoon over: the class couple, the couple who has been dating since college, the best friends who decided to date. They've been together for years, and everyone wonders why they are not planning a future, living together yet, or engaged. You've seen these relationships; you may even envy them. But then, out of the blue you learn that they didn't stay together.

"What happened?" Everyone is left wide-eyed with mouths agape. Friends and family members are shocked until the dust settles, details are leaked, and the problems in the relationship they both tried to ignore inevitably float to the surface. You know why people are shocked? Because we all want to believe the fairy tale. Hell, I hope you live it. But you can't live within the pages of a story that wasn't written for you. Believe me. I tried.

At twenty-seven, the year I declared I would be married, I was alone. I was broken. The final blow came when rumors flew that he was flirting with girls at his new job. True or untrue didn't matter. When I questioned the rumors, he spun a tale about how I didn't trust him and, because of that, he couldn't be in a relationship with me any longer. He couldn't believe I dared to question his loyalty, character, and decision-making.

I fell for it and beat myself up for over a year. I combed over the relationship and highlighted moments where I could have been better. I spent too long wishing I could have done something to stop the role I played in the breakup and the pain that we both endured in the aftermath.

Within a month or two of our tragic end, he was already in a serious relationship. While I had to drag myself to work and deliver *The Canterbury Tale*s to a bunch of teenagers who would rather pluck their eyelashes out than read "The Knight's Tale," he was happy. I had to appear stable. I wasn't. I had to pretend that I was whole so my students didn't see me break. I was their teacher, after all, not a real person.

So I did what I always did. I taught my ass off. My students never knew I was in pain. Because that's the thing about your teacher. He or she is there to serve you. But, that year, those kids served me. My classroom became my safe place. A place where the pain disappeared and I was me. It was the only place where love didn't leave me. I hope you have these special places and that you have learned these places can also be within.

The reality of this time still makes me sad. I am sad for the younger version of myself who wore her heart on her sleeve and carried insecurity and fear like two 500-pound weights on her back. I am sad, because I know if he asked, I would have married him. I know, too, that somewhere in my gut I would have known it was wrong, but I would have accepted it. I fought to fix it in fact. And I am grateful that Tommy didn't let me.

This gratitude took time. The truth is, back then, I hated him because I couldn't stop loving him and my heart was so broken. Tommy wasn't my first love, but I put my whole future in his hands, so when he walked away, I felt completely lost. I felt crashing emotions of the various stages of grief like a wild tornado deep inside from the minute I opened my eyes in the morning until I cried myself to sleep at night. This went on for months with no relief from the pain.

Depression: it can lurk around casting a shadow that you can't seem to escape and then like an ugly beast it sits on your chest and is so heavy it's hard to breathe. It's something I've seen sitting in my classroom, plaguing my students, and driving them to seek assistance. The reasons vary, but the signs are recognizable: loss of interest in school and friends, grades slipping, increased absences, silence, to name a few. Depression doesn't care if you're popular, wealthy, gorgeous, or smart. If it wants to sit on you, it will. You might not be able to get up, but if someone offers to help you stand, reach for them.

When I finally took the leap to see my first therapist, it was with the support of my friend Nikki and my mom. I wept as I took the initial survey that offered feedback concerning my mental state. I remember struggling to be honest. On a scale of 1 to 10, daily feelings like hopelessness and sadness were at an all-time high: 10. Did I have thoughts of suicide? I'd be lying if I didn't admit that at this time death seemed less painful. I even believed that his death would have been easier to cope with than being left and knowing he moved on.

As hard as it is to revisit this dark time, it's more important to me that you know I was here, and here I am now. Time passes, things change, and hearts heal. How you choose to spend the time in between is a choice. With support, you can grow out of darkness and find light again.

I was diagnosed with depression, and after months of feeling paralyzed and tearful, I was prescribed medication to help me see beyond the sadness. Taking medication and feeling like I couldn't control my emotions was another uneasy step for me, but with support, I found the courage to nurture my mental health. And yes, courage is the right word. Because when you look at yourself in the mirror and see someone you don't recognize, looking away is far easier than facing the pain you see.

I knew it was time for me to explore this option because some days it felt like I couldn't get out of bed even though I hardly slept. When I did close my eyes, I found myself shaking with anxiety and panic about my future. Thankfully, in time, talk therapy and medication helped these feelings to subside and helped clear the thick fog and dark shadows that settled in around me. Day by day, it became slightly easier to move forward.

Every morning when the bell rang, somehow I snapped out of the darkness and slipped into the role of your funny, caring English teacher. I was in control, and I didn't miss a beat. In many ways, the bell saved me. One lesson at a time I healed. In fact, I didn't just heal; in time, I actually found myself again. The girl who loved her friends, who loved her students, who loved to write, and read, and trusted herself. I found the girl I wasn't when I was with him. I reunited with the version of myself I allowed him to overshadow. I learned the right relationship should always, and I mean always, keep you in the sun.

I do not wish heartbreak on any of you, but I have learned that, without it, we do not truly know how to appreciate the right love. So don't be afraid to get your heart broken, go ahead and lose yourself in someone else for all the right reasons, and then come up for air, look around, and try to see your-self from the outside and take a long, thoughtful look within. I hope you see yourself there, happy, whole, and intact. But if you see yourself slipping away, and your heart eventually breaks, know this simple truth: your heart will heal. You will find yourself falling in love again. And that heartbreak will help guide you safely where you are meant to land in love and stay.

Objective: Throw Spaghetti

I f you throw enough spaghetti at the wall, eventually something will stick." These were the words of advice from my first therapist, Leslie. I continued to talk to her about being lonely and continued to stress that I would never find love again or have the chance to live the life that I really wanted. She simply said to start throwing spaghetti. But here's the thing about throwing spaghetti: it takes time to cook and won't stick until it's just right.

Throwing spaghetti is what has to happen in order to get what you really long for in this life.

In others words, you have to try. Trying can and often does result in many, many failed attempts. For me, this meant I was going to have to go out and start dating again. For you, throwing spaghetti might mean something different, but if you really want something, you have to go for it.

Sure. It's important to be proud of where you are now and what you have already accomplished, but if something is pulling at your heart, listen. Of course, it's easier to go back to what you know or search for alternatives to what you really desire. These options all sound safer than facing potential failure on your way to what you really want and absolutely deserve, but are you okay with never knowing what else, or always wondering what if?

Picture yourself completely famished in your favorite restaurant. It's Friday night and you can't wait to enjoy a great meal with friends. You're really not in the mood for chicken. But you know you love the way the chef makes and presents his version of chicken scarpariello. The chicken is served on the bone, just like your grandmother used to make it. You know as soon as you lightly pierce it with your fork, the tender meat will slide off the bone. The potatoes are served around the chicken and rest perfectly in the pan juices that remain from the sweet and savory mixture of onions and a variety of sweet and hot peppers. But chicken? You just had chicken yesterday.

You never tried the steak pizzaiola. But what if you don't enjoy it? You are so hungry, you're not sure you want to chance leaving your favorite spot disappointed. Life is so busy, who knows when you will have the chance to get there again. The server circles around for the second time to take your order and asks, "What can I get you?"

"I'll take the chicken scarpariello," you respond, the same way you always do at your favorite spot, and your buddy laughs.

"I could have told her that the first time she came by." He pokes fun at your predictability and you just shrug. No chance taken. No risk. You're satisfied and content. But, man, you're getting sick of chicken. Are you getting this? Or just getting hungry?

You see, this is why many people stay in jobs they hate and in relationships that aren't satisfying. This is why people keep ordering the chicken, because sticking to what you know feels safer. This being said, you better really love that chicken scarpariello because you are making a choice by not making a choice to try something else.

Before I dared to throw spaghetti, I spent a long time looking back and searching for viable alternatives to putting my heart back on the line. I hoped maybe Tommy would realize what a terrible mistake he had made and call. Dead silence. Hmm. Maybe I will meet someone again at work. Eye roll. Head shake. No. Never again. Maybe I am meant to be just a really cool, rich aunt with an extravagant lifestyle. But I am a high school teacher. And I assure you being the varsity cheerleading coach at a high school does not come with a Land Rover, private jet, or beachfront property. I was trying to convince myself that living a life without someone to share it with would work for me. I kept ordering chicken. Are you following this?

When I finally came to terms with the truth that none of these ideas were going to satisfy my search for companionship, I took my boiling pot of spaghetti and started to throw. I suggest that you do too. Note: Throwing spaghetti doesn't have to be a drastic all-in move at first. There are many ways to step toward what you truly desire without uprooting your life, quitting your job, breaking up with your boyfriend, or never eating chicken again.

Think about it, why not order the chicken and commit to sharing half of it with your friend who is willing to order that steak you had your eye on. If throwing spaghetti with all your might scares you, try tossing it at first. If you really want something, resolve yourself in the fact that it may take time to get it. And it's going to be uncomfortable.

Start Kissing Frogs

I'll admit, I took the easy route at first. I have many friends, and when your friends are in relationships, they want you to be happy too. It's just like finding a prom date. You know, your friend is going with her boyfriend, so of course it would be just perfect if you could go with her boyfriend's friend. Sometimes, it really is this easy and works. People tell these stories all the time. They gush as their story ends with a wide, toothy smile and the big reveal, as if we didn't see it coming, "—and then we got married!" Other times, your friend found the diamond in the rough of the whole friend group and all that's left is, well, the rough. But because I promised my therapist I would throw some spaghetti, I stuck my hand in the boiling pot and grabbed whatever I could find.

Let me start this by saying I love my friends. But I found myself questioning their dating choices for me: *Really? This guy? Do you hate me?*

Krista was friends with a guy we will call Jacob. I have known Krista since I was five years old. I was there when she lost her baby teeth. I stood next to her at preschool graduation. I was there when she had her first kiss. I was there when she got her driver's license. I was there when she left for college. I stood by her side when she got married. You see what I'm getting at?

I don't know where this Jacob guy came from. I probably should have asked, but I was committed to throwing spaghetti. So when Krista and her husband said they would fix me up with a friend and promised to come on a double date for support, I half-heartedly took hold of that slippery piece of pasta, tossed it out there, and hoped it stuck.

Keeping commitments many times must precede emotion. Be honest, most days, do you really feel like going to school? How about the hours of homework you completed when you were exhausted from school, sports, and hanging with friends? Life is full of things you may not feel like doing, like stopping for gas when it's freezing out, or showing up for your annual dental appointment. Sure, you could refuse to do any of these things, but then you can't act surprised if you find yourself stalled on the side of the road with a gnarly set of teeth.

If I didn't do things I didn't feel like doing, every student I ever taught would have an A and

I'd never grade one paper. That being said, I'd also be a horrible teacher. This book would also still be stuck in my computer, unfinished. Sometimes, you just don't feel like putting in the effort or risking an unfavorable consequence, but experience teaches that keeping commitments and staying consistent leads to success.

I applied this same principle to my dating life and met Krista, her husband, and Jacob for a night out. And just like that I was dating again. Dinner was pleasant. The food was delicious. The conversation with Jacob was mediocre at best. He was trying too hard to impress me with accomplishments I did not find impressive like his success, his money, and how he never learned to be humble. I didn't really learn much about his family, passions, or background. I felt no spark, but I was with my friends, so I was having fun. I was doing it. I was taking a chance and it felt good to be semi out of my comfort zone trying to find love again.

"I got it on my first try!" People yell this when it happens because it's unique. *Beginner's luck.* Same idea. Most of you will learn that it's perfectly noble to have failed attempts on your life's résumé. It's the norm. Baseball allows three strikes. Football allows four downs. Most goals will take more than one shot, or more than one piece of spaghetti, to win.

I had a student years ago who declared she was only applying to one college. As you can imagine, I was concerned and questioned why she made the decision to limit her options.

"Did you talk to your guidance counselor?" I pushed. "What do your parents think about that?" I couldn't understand why, if she really wanted to go to college, she would limit her options to one school. Why would she take one shot when most games aren't won this way?

She convinced herself that if she didn't get into her dream school, she wasn't going. Well, guess what happened? Correct. When the rejection came, she scrambled to figure out what she really wanted. Turned out, it wasn't the school she really wanted; it was the goal of becoming a nurse. So she quickly fished out another piece of spaghetti and threw it. In fact, she kept throwing until she found herself accepted into a reputable nursing program that fall. There is no other alternative. You either process the loss and keep throwing, or you spend your life watching opportunity boil and eventually fall apart.

You know the expression: get back on that horse. For one of my students this was literally the problem. Horseback riding had always played a massive role in her life, and in her happiness. Her love for horses even provided her a place she felt safe with people who became her closest friends. Yet, jumping back into competitive horseback riding after suffering a traumatic fall during a horse show left her second-guessing her ability to return to the sport she once loved. This moment put fear in a place that was previously one of safety flooded with nothing but joy and satisfaction.

It was time for her to rethink what she always knew. It took time for her to adjust her mindset, but she committed months to rebuilding her trust and confidence in the relationship with her horse. When she was ready to reenter the world of competitive horseback riding, she and her horse entered a more prestigious show with a fresh attitude; together they left the painful experience in their rearview. You see, the spaghetti that falls can make room for you to grow before trying again.

After my cameo back into the dating world with Jacob, I, too, dipped my hand back in the boiling pot, as I continued to throw spaghetti with intention. I agreed to go out on another blind date. Looking back, I should have requested more than "I know a guy" as a prerequisite for agreeing to go on these blind dates. But like I said, I am loyal, and I keep promises. At this point in my life, I was committed to throwing spaghetti. If I got burned, well,

I was willing to take the chance. Slowly, my mind-set was refocusing on the goal.

This guy we will call Giovanni. I am of 100 percent Italian descent. My grandma, a first-generation American, always prided herself on saying she was an American. This being said, I always imagined myself with a man who had a similar background, but never found myself in a serious relationship with an Italian. So when the opportunity to date a man named Giovanni popped up, I thought maybe the luck of the Irish did not pertain to me, because our roots were so different. Eureka! I cracked the code!

Seriously, I had this thought. I was this desperate to figure out why I was still single and searching. It was like being the last to find a prom date in high school. That was me, too, by the way. But this time the deadline was heavy. The deadline was not some onetime dance or sorority date party with a guy I may or may not see ever again. The deadline now was lasting love.

It's important to stop here and mention that although these deadlines may feel real, they are all made up. Ignore the urge to give in to an imaginary time stamp on your life. Most of these deadlines are rooted in a fantasy that life will be easy and we have total control over everything life throws in front of us. This is not the case. The truth is, if we did have total control, life would be boring.

Also, side note: I didn't have my first serious boyfriend until I was in college. And I fully support this story. High school sweethearts happen, don't get me wrong. But they also come with challenges. I have seen this all unfold in different ways, and the only truth that I know for sure is we have absolutely no control over when forever love finds us. Trust me. I'm living proof of this truth, but now back to Giovanni's moment in this story and how it will help you throw spaghetti or rather start to be selective on what you choose to throw.

He was an electrician. We spoke briefly on the phone, and within minutes I was attracted to his thick city accent. His voice reminded me of my mom's first cousins; his voice sounded like my aunt Gloria's kitchen on a Sunday afternoon. He was loud, funny, and enthusiastic. My mind painted him as Ray Liotta in *Goodfellas*; I imagined he was sexy and maybe a little daring and perhaps dangerous. It was classic "nice girl goes for bad boy" nonsense, but I found myself excited to throw this piece of spaghetti.

He picked me up in his white Mercedes. I knew he was outside, because I could hear a loud thump getting louder and louder as his car got closer to my condo. Granted I did live in a quiet, suburban neighborhood, but it also sounded like a storm was approaching. Little did I know that was exactly what was heading toward me.

We had dinner reservations at an Italian restaurant near my house. So, as I saw him, correction, heard him pull up, I ran out to meet him. When I got in, the car was completely black inside. And by black I mean there were no interior lights at all. It was a total blackout even when he started the car. There wasn't even a light on the speedometer. How did he know how fast he was driving? And why did I get in his car? You see, selective spaghetti, my friends. Selective spaghetti.

Before I could ask any questions, or second-guess my decision to let him drive, he turned on the music. It was just as loud as it was when he pulled up the street, but from the inside, it felt like I was stuck standing near the speaker at a concert. As if that wasn't bad enough, the dash where the music was coming from suddenly lit up and shot several strobe lights of color. The lights bounced around the car to the beat of techno music. I swear I was in a club on four wheels.

We pulled down the street and I was speechless, which was good because there was no way he could have heard a word I had to say anyway. The last straw was when he lit a cigarette and didn't bother to roll down a window. Yup, I thought, this car is a club, a club I wish I didn't get into, and there was no sign of the nearest exit. I could feel the spaghetti slipping down the wall.

Dinner was painful. Don't get me wrong, the food was delicious, but I could barely eat. I was too busy looking around trying to make eye contact with people dining nearby hoping my eyes communicated an apology. He was talking like Tony Soprano at the restaurant. His use of profanity and slang made me beyond uncomfortable; at one point I had to ask him to lower his voice. The people at the table next to us kept glancing over, and rightfully so, they were irritated. I did my best not to slide under the table when he used a racial slur. This date was over before it even started. Another piece of miserably cold, wet, and undercooked pasta fell. I felt this one drop with a sigh of relief.

That's what happens when you take chances and have a few misses. You start to relax and accept the process. How can this awful date help you to reach in and throw spaghetti? The truth is: It can't, and that's the point. It was not worth my time to throw this piece of spaghetti. You should throw with intention and be mindful of the actual opportunity in front of you. You see, the minute I learned about Giovanni, I started to make assumptions about him and how he would make sense in my life. Assumptions may cause you to assign value and time to a situation that doesn't prove to deserve it or you.

Similar to the way my former student fantasized about a nursing school that didn't offer her a spot, I let my imagination take my heart to a place that never existed. I was ready to glue this piece of spaghetti to the wall before I even touched it. Throwing spaghetti in desperation never works.

Sometimes it takes time to realize that while throwing spaghetti you may need to shut the stove off completely and take a step back to assess your approach. Like most endeavors, the right timing is of the essence. One of my seniors intended on applying to art school and was working on her portfolio to showcase her best work to prove her potential. Her body of work after being evaluated would determine whether she was accepted or rejected. Like it happens in most creative fields, this process is competitive and requires dedication and a willingness to dig in and accept critique in order to improve before submission. My student found herself paralyzed by the gravity of the end result and struggled to open her sketchbook or pick up her colored pencils.

Frustration, anger, and panic quickly colored her ability to approach her work. Constant reminders from her teacher and of course the looming deadlines did not help. It was like a literal block stood between her and her creative ability. She tried to break through several times, but her attempts produced uninspired work and showed little improvement on her existing creations.

She realized it was time to surrender her weapons. Hands up. Pencils down. She stepped away from her blank and half-completed canvases that stood taunting her and decided to silence them for an entire week. She cleared her head and pushed through her frustration to make room for new techniques that eventually ignited her passion to step up and create. With just a moment of breathing room, and a new approach, she quickly received artistic validation that she was making meaningful steps to her goal.

You see, sometimes throwing spaghetti the same way over and over is the reason it is not sticking. You can't keep throwing spaghetti the same way and expect different results. It's like trying out for the baseball team every spring and wondering why you never make it, yet you refuse to touch a bat or throw a ball all winter while everyone else puts in time at the batting cage and plays on a travel team. Sooner or later, it becomes clear that it's time to adjust your strategy.

While it was comfortable to share my dating attempts with close friends, and often helpful to have their recommendations, it was time to start throwing spaghetti on my own. The friends of friends method was proving to be a bit of a disaster. Here was *my* strategy: I would go out with my girlfriends, go straight to the bar, and choose the bartender who was the friendliest and best looking. Pathetic, I know. But at this time in my life, I was working my way out of a dark place. You opened my book. I'm cheering for you; don't judge me. Besides, this method worked twice. Okay, it also ended twice. But one of these bartenders actually taught me something. You're welcome.

I recognized him from college. He ran in the same Greek circle as I did, and we quickly reconnected as he served me and my friends drinks. I know, I'm getting predictable here. But I couldn't resist. When I was a freshman, he was completely out of my league. At twenty-eight though, it all evened out. I thought he surely had potential. My sorority sisters confirmed; this guy was a good idea.

He grabbed my number and we met out a few nights later. He was cute and funny and he was starting his first job as an English teacher that

September. Things just seemed to click. You know what I mean, I'm sure. Cue the fireworks.

At the end of the date he charmingly said good-bye and that he liked to end great dates early so there was something to look forward to. I loved that idea, and in the same breath he confirmed his feelings were mutual and that there would be a second date. I left thinking this piece of spaghetti just might stick.

Do You Love Yourself?

Hope is how you continue to try even in the wake of failure. The smallest sign that you are on the right track can give you the encouragement you need to continue taking steps toward what you really want. When you look up from throwing spaghetti, you should start to feel proud of where you've been and that includes the moments that left you second-guessing yourself, rolling your eyes, and shaking your head. Why? Because if you keep going despite the heartbreak and disappointment, it's because you love yourself enough to trust that what you deserve will find its way to you when you are truly ready to receive it.

On our second date, he said he had a surprise for me. He picked me up and told me we were going to an amusement park. Super sweet, right? According to a barrel of rom-coms, we were going to hold hands walking around the park and maybe share a funnel cake or cotton candy. He would win a huge teddy bear for me by throwing darts at a wall of balloons, or by swinging a sledge hammer until we heard the bell ring at the top of the strength tester. It had all the ingredients of the perfect date. Well, until he pulled the car over on the highway and told me he was sorry, but he had something to tell me.

With my stomach in a twist and my mind swirling like a fidget spinner, I turned, faced him, and waited for the news. He then proceeded to tell me he was a member of a white supremacy group. When my face turned white, his face broke into a smile and he said he was only kidding; he was just a recovering alcoholic. I learned that managing someone's questionable relationship with alcohol was not something I should have been willing to do again. But because I was so lonely, and once again needed him to boost my self-esteem, I hung in there until he decided the relationship wasn't for him. I learned that I was still willing to take less than I was giving. Thankfully, despite my attempts to hold it in place, another piece of spaghetti slid hopelessly down the wall.

Over a year went by and all I had to show for it was a floor of wet, uncooked spaghetti. I even tried online dating. After I showed Nikki the bio I published, she laughed and said, "Whose profile is this?" Apparently, it sounded nothing like me. My profile was littered with superficial facts about my life and portrayed my journey to find love as relaxed and casual. It had no mention of my true desire to fall in love, settle down, and have a family. There was no focus on what actually mattered like true character, life goals, and mutual respect.

You may have some friends who tell you what you want to hear. You may have friends who smile and nod politely when you have an idea or spew some bullshit as a defense mechanism to protect your ego. Nikki is not this friend. You need these people in your life too. She got right in my face and said I needed to stop worrying so much about what guys looked like and start worrying about their personalities. Her actual words, "You need a good guy, not an asshole."

Well, I certainly didn't need a computer to help me find the wrong guy; I was doing that just fine on my own. This was the first time anyone ever challenged me to confront my truth. Nikki knew I was searching for a guy who would help hide my insecurity. I was searching for a replacement for

Tommy. I was stuck in the "if he was cool, I was cool by association" high school bullshit.

As you are reading this, you may be currently stuck too. You may be really cool or at least people see you this way, so you are living up to their expectations. Maybe you are dressing the part. Maybe you are burning the hell out of your hair every morning and gluing on eyelashes or hair extensions to look like that Instafamous girl you believe has the perfect life. Maybe you are taking supplements or working out to the point of exhaustion, because you are too small or too big to be what you think you are supposed to be.

If you are not doing some version of this, bravo! You are way ahead of most of us. Because it's high school, and it's normal to try out a bunch of stuff searching for what fits or at least what or who will help you fit in. This is high school, but it can also be any other time in your life when insecurity and doubt rear their ugly heads.

Sure, I was throwing spaghetti, but I was really looking for someone to be a reflection of how I wanted to be seen. Searching for someone or something that makes you look better than you feel inside is wasted energy toward a superficial goal. After many, many failed attempts it became clear that this is not how you look for love. This is not how you find who you are meant to marry. Hell. This isn't even how you should date or make friends. EVER. Any goal that you are trying to reach for the sake of others or for optics will surely leave you dissatisfied. The truth is, no one cares what your life "looks" like. What matters is your genuine happiness.

I needed to be enough all by myself before I could fall in love again. How could I attempt to give myself to someone else when I didn't even have enough love for myself? On paper I looked great. On the outside I was young, fun, and joy riding through a charmed life in a blue luxury convertible. I looked great, but inside I was still feeling insecure and uncomfortable, chunky, with big curly hair and glasses. I had to love this girl and embrace her before I could expect anyone else to love me the way I deserved to be loved. This is not the exception. This is the rule. Love works when you love yourself and that especially includes the unfiltered, ugly stuff.

I had no choice but to let my spaghetti simmer and continue to work on myself until I was ready to reach in the boiling pot and try again. Don't be afraid to let your spaghetti simmer, too, even if it feels like everyone around you is already dressed up, settled in their seats at the table, and ready to eat. There is no rush. Your person, your goal, and your deepest desire does not deserve an under-cooked meal and neither do you. But when it's right, and when you're truly ready, go ahead, reach in, grab as much spaghetti as you can—and throw.

Lesson 10

Objective:
Let It Stick

It was the end of June—the time of year when most students only come into school for local final exams or state tests and teachers are holed up in hot, sticky classrooms grading papers. This is the time of year I now refer to as Vegas. I spend most days entering numbers into my online grade book, pretending to pull the handle on a slot machine, and silently screaming, "Come on, 65!" Where 65 signifies a passing grade. Jackpot! This number means credits are granted and diplomas are awarded.

Believe it or not, your teachers want you to pass; we hate when students fail. June is also the time of year I start counting the minutes until the school year is over. Yes, your teachers can't wait for the school year to end either. You may not know this, but teachers can be worse than students. In June, we too have Senioritis; we are tapped out. Exhausted. So when I was interrupted by a phone call about yet another blind date, I was less than enthusiastic.

It's like the teacher who assigns work or expects you to pay attention the day before winter break. I don't care how old you are, your head is in another place, and it's tough to muster up the energy to pretend to care. That's how it can feel when you find yourself tired from throwing spaghetti. But like that teacher who will fail you if you don't hand in that ten-page paper everyone thought was unreasonable, your future depends on how you step up when you see an opportunity that has the potential to change your future.

That spring, throwing spaghetti had been slow, and my mother's words, no matter how I tried to silence them, rang in my ear: "You're not going to meet anyone sitting at home." She was painfully right. You might as well settle into this reality too. Your mother, or whoever you see as a mother figure, has a way of knowing what she is talking about, even when you hate hearing it. *Take your vitamins.*

Get some rest. You need to study. Clean your room. Did you take out the garbage? Say thank you. For the love of God, you need a shower. Sorry. But it's all true. Every last annoying command.

Exhale and get on board.

I listened as my brother's wife gushed with excitement about this setup, and I couldn't help but be intrigued by the proposition of going to a wedding. A wedding? Yes, a wedding. The blind date up for consideration was to go to a wedding with a guy I didn't know. At. All.

You know where this is going right? But here's why. When my nephew was born, you know the one I told you about who wanted to be the Incredible Hulk, this customer named John stopped in the hair salon where my brother's wife worked and dropped off a musical frog as a gift. The frog was about two feet tall and wore a straw hat and a bowtie. When my nephew pushed on the frog's foot, the frog's head moved back and forth and it sang "What a Wonderful World," you know the version sung by Louis Armstrong. It was an adorable gift, and the girls in the salon swooned over this thoughtful, single fireman with blue eyes.

This frog is what ultimately convinced me to go on a blind date to a wedding, where I knew no one. Even as I write these words I am shocked.

Seriously, what was I thinking? And seriously, how did I pull myself together so fast? Sometimes you'll find yourself throwing spaghetti you didn't expect to reach for, but for some reason, you can't explain, your heart will scream, "Let's go!"

Recently, I met a podcaster in his midtwenties. We started chatting about life after high school, and he sheepishly admitted that college wasn't his path after he graduated. It was surprising when he revealed that he left home and took off without a plan to live in Montana to, as he explained, find himself.

Montana? What? Why? This was the reaction from his family, which explained the hesitation when he told his story. However, without taking this chance to explore a place he never knew, he is convinced that today his life would be completely different. Sure. He eventually moved back East and decided to pursue a college degree, but the motivation and passion to pursue his degree in creative writing is completely fueled by his unexpected experiences of life in Montana—a piece of spaghetti he didn't know he had to throw to get him where he wanted to stay.

Sometimes, spaghetti chooses you. I was going to this wedding, with or without my consent. My number was already passed along to firefighter

John and the girls in the salon had already said, "Sure! She'll go."

Another classic example of how, when you are single, everyone has the perfect guy, girl, solution, and date to heal your broken heart whether you ask for help or not. The simple reason is because these people love you. During this time in my life, I leaned on my friends more than ever. I was blessed with a team of women who truly wanted to see me happy and couldn't wait to stand by my side when I finally found my forever. These are the same women who love my children and still stand by my side. Did they think this particular blind date was crazy? Probably, but they cheered me on anyway. These are the people you hold close to you—always.

You don't need an army. High school, unfortunately might set you up to believe quantity matters. Social media isn't helping this narrative either. But, right now, when you think about your friends, consider: Who really loves you? Who accepts you when you're up and down? Who remembers your birthday and all the other reasons life gives you to celebrate? Who checks on you and hears you even when you say nothing? These people are rare and valuable. And when you're throwing spaghetti, these are the people who will truly rejoice when it sticks.

Your Time Will Come

Truth be told, I was excited and nervous about reaching in the pot and throwing this piece of spaghetti. This blind date may have been a hard no a year prior, but like I said, time changes everything and time heals. Such a simple concept: Wait. Be patient and all will be well. But when you're in it, I mean neck deep in a tough time, no matter how true it may be, who the hell wants to wait for things to take their natural course?

Tick. Tick. Tick. A sweet young man waited his whole life to be honest about his sexuality. It was his junior year, and he finally decided to let his true voice be heard. He hoped his final years of high school would finally allow him to live as his authentic self. He shared that he was gay in his school community, and although he felt relieved at first, it didn't take long before he overheard hurtful comments and criticism. Fear of the reaction that kept him silent was exactly what he received.

Already feeling vulnerable and in a fragile state made it extremely difficult to tick, tick, tick through the pain. So he fell silently back into pretending to be a heterosexual male despite his truth. You should know that his time will come, too, just like yours will. The time will come when his truth will take precedence over meaningless opinions from people who don't matter. Waiting is hard, and sometimes painful, but time can provide courage, perspective, and strength, if you let it.

Trust the process. How many times have you seen this sentiment pop up on your social media feed, hammered onto a piece of jewelry, or tattooed across some guy's collar bone in the gym? You know what you don't see anyone advertising? That the process is often long and challenging.

While I waited for John to call with the details of the blind date. I couldn't help but share my Friday night plans with my colleague who was married with two children. It was no surprise that he didn't think this date was such a smart idea. He joked that John could be a complete psychopath. Looking back he absolutely had a valid point, and I probably should have considered this possibility, but I was twenty-eight. And twenty-eight-year-olds are not thirty or forty and are still haphazardly dancing between daring, dumb, and wise, so I took a shot, and you should too. Be safe, of course, but this is what throwing spaghetti is all about. How else can you figure out what is supposed to stick?

You pick a major and eventually a career and hope it sticks. The goal is to find a career that doesn't feel like work. News flash: It all feels like work sometimes, but finding your niche—the place where you are happy to do the work—is the goal.

Imagine: My former student graduates with a four-year degree in design from an expensive private school. But as she works through the demanding process of constructing a collection and finishing her degree, she realizes a great need for mental health support in the grueling world of the fashion industry. Previous struggles with anxiety and depression popped up again, and she just knew in her gut that she wanted to work for a company that truly helped people, not just created a facade of support for marketability. She trusted her instinct and decided to brainstorm how she could help fill this hole in an industry that didn't often cater to or address mental health awareness.

Starting a brand that donates 10 percent of its proceeds to advocate for mental health while still working a full-time job is the epitome of taking a risk fueled by the heart. This type of endeavor could be a massive failure, or her clothing line could blow up and become the next GAP, Under Armour, Lululemon, or whatever other brand you love because of the visible logo sewed on the front.

The point is nothing sticks without taking a shot. She is driven by her passion to help people and make a difference in a space that calls her to serve. While she started the brand to help others, this risk has been a gift in her life as well, and just like that she found what was meant to stick.

That hot day in June when John finally called, I could barely hear him. It sounded like he was driving through a tunnel or riding in a garbage truck. Why? Because he was working a second job driving a garbage truck. He said when he was done he would pick me up so we could go to his friend's wedding.

"Uh. That's okay. I can meet you at your house," I said as I quickly took control. I was getting braver and more daring at throwing spaghetti, but I wasn't stupid. After my experience with Giovanni, and the smoky club on wheels, I learned to keep my getaway car close at all times. Did I mention that time also teaches?

John rattled off the plans in a confident, friendly, enthusiastic, masculine tone and my night was set. I just needed to leave work, take a shower, do my hair and makeup, and, of course, self-talk my way into being a confident, spontaneous dater and put on the dress. Cue the anxiety!

If you haven't even dipped your toe in the calming ocean that ebbs and flows off the beaches of positive self-talk, you better book a trip fast. What you tell yourself as you find what works for you will make a tremendous difference in your journey. Affirmations. Mantras. Credos. Declarations. I don't care what you call these voices in your head, but keep them in line, and tell them to shut the hell up if they try to ruin your vibe while preparing to throw spaghetti.

The dress was sky blue and turquoise, and it was only worn once before the night I met John for the first time. I'm not even sure if John knows the backstory of the dress I wore on the night our story started. But here's the thing: When you meet someone, anyone, whether that person becomes your person or not, he or she has a backstory. We all do. Some of the details of these backstories are the most beautiful parts of who we become and how we grow into new relationships. And some details suck.

That's it. I wish I had a better word. A more poetic way of saying it, but we all can relate to what I'm talking about here. Sure. We cling to clichés like *everything happens for a reason,* and *what doesn't kill you makes you stronger,* thank you, Kelly Clarkson. But at the end of the day, sometimes the tough stuff just sucks. So here it is.

The last time I was with football coach Tommy, we had already broken up, but in the spirit of maturity we had committed to attend a mutual friend's wedding together. At the time, I was still holding onto a thread of hope that we had a chance at reconciliation, so I went out that morning to search for a dress that would convince Tommy he couldn't live without me. I spent the morning shopping and praying I would find the perfect blue dress. I prayed directly to my grandma Evelyn who had passed when I was in high school. She was a strong, independent figure in my life, who, like my maternal grandmother, lost her husband too soon and was living proof that life goes on, laughter continues, and joy can be found again.

That morning, just when I was about to give up the search for a dress that would give me the boost of confidence I needed, I saw a blue piece of material peeping out of a packed sale rack in the back of a chain clothing store at the mall. It was my size and exactly what I was looking for. It was a blue, lightweight, one shoulder dress, and it did what I needed it to do, even if it wasn't what I wanted at the time.

That night, Tommy did slip back into us, and he admitted that he still loved me, but as we said goodbye, it was clear that he was done and that night was the last time we would be together. It was days later when I found out he had already been in another relationship. That dress was with me when Tommy broke my heart for the last time.

So when I pulled it out the evening of my blind date with John, I took a deep breath and exhaled. I remember hoping maybe this dress was found for a much more important reason than falling back into a love that wasn't working. You don't know until you know why life unfolds the way it does. Do your best to navigate with hope always riding shotgun.

No Bad Days

My first impression of John: Wow, he has some spiked hair. Holy blue eyes, and is this guy husband material? First impressions matter, but I've learned they also lead to assumptions about people, and when you're trying to get spaghetti to stick, assumptions will get in your way.

How many times has an assumption tripped you up? In order to really go for it, whatever goal you may be working toward, you have to leave your desire to fill-in-the-blanks out of it.

"How many of each animal did Adam bring on his ark?"

"Two," many students proudly shout out from their seats.

"How many months of the year have twenty-eight days?"

"Only one!" Inevitably a student confidently responds. We have a good laugh when I repeat the questions and they take a minute to reconsider.

They all know it was Noah's ark, not Adam's, and they certainly realize all twelve months have twenty-eight days. However, the instinct to fill in what they know and cling to the familiar doesn't allow for the possibility that they are missing what is actually in front of them. This is how my colleagues and I teach the probable pitfalls of making assumptions. In this lesson, the only thing at stake is a brief moment of embarrassment, coupled with an eye roll, and a head shake. However, if you take this same approach while throwing spaghetti, the results could be much more impactful.

Unfortunately, we do this all the time when we meet new people. And, yes, I did this with John. Think back to the first time you met your current partner, or your best friend, or the first time you stepped into a new class and met a new teacher. How many of these first impressions told you all you needed to know? How much did you assume that was later proven wrong? It's natural to walk into a new situation or meet new people and put it or them into a nice neat file folder that feels familiar.

This filing method does not work when you're trying to get spaghetti to stick. You see, the point of this chapter is for you to understand that in order to find what's truly right for you, you have to be willing to let go of what you know and approach new chances to throw spaghetti with an open mind and a willingness to let what is for you unfold.

No Bad Days written in white next to two palm trees was the sentiment stuck on the rear window of John's truck, and it seemed to match his demeanor perfectly. His presence felt fresh and easy. I was surprisingly comfortable riding next to him, and my nerves started to relax immediately. It helped that he smelled like a swirl of soap and clean cologne. He was so casual and charismatic, it was rubbing off on me. *Well, this is new,* I thought.

As he pulled down his driveway, he asked if I picked up a card. *What?* He started to laugh, but what was actually funny, I think he was dead serious. We made a quick stop, picked up a card, and he handed it to me to fill out. This shined a light on the reality that I was really doing this: going to a wedding where I knew no one, not even my date. I had to ask, "What are their names?" And then the worst part, "How do you spell your name? Is it J-o-n or J-o-h-n?" He didn't seem bothered at all and continued to treat me like we had history.

Do self-checks. Spaghetti sticks best when you feel like yourself in the moment. You know why colleges insist you set up a visit and attend a tour? Because this is the time when they can lull you into a feeling of comfort and belonging. You either feel it or you don't. If you feel like you fit while on campus, you're more likely to apply, take out student loans, or throw your entire college fund their way. Cha-ching. Mission accomplished.

This moment of self-check works every time. Think of all the people, places, and things you love. Most likely they have one thing in common: they all make you feel good. That's why they are part of your life. That's why they stick—effortlessly.

"We just met!" I answered repeatedly when people asked how long John and I have been dating as we walked through the cocktail hour like a couple. It was quite funny as we all laughed at the absurdity of the situation. Shortly after, the bride and groom were introduced for the first time, and everyone in the room stood up to congratulate them. Well everyone except for John. He was comfortable in his chair eating his salad and just said, "They won't care if I don't stand up," and he laughed, which made me laugh, and together we stood up and clapped for this couple who reminded me love is possible.

Anything's Possible

It's easy to forget this when throwing spaghetti gets hard. But if you are open to this truth, your world will provide reminders every day. I left work on a Thursday due to COVID and thought, naively like many of us did, that I was in for a long weekend while school districts disinfected. Little did any of us know that first shutdown would change our world for so much longer—and in some cases perhaps forever. How could teaching from home be possible? How could students get what they needed with no access to a physical space and little access to teachers? How were students supposed to obtain credit for classes and move forward when school was closed with no date of reentry?

This was one of the greatest challenges I've faced as a teacher. I would imagine you were in the trenches, too, maybe feeling alone or lost and doubting that your education even had a fighting chance to continue. But you see, during this time what we all had was possibility. Nobody had the answers, so spaghetti started flying. Google classroom, Zoom, voice recordings, videos, emails, and countless other creative methods to teach lessons to students who never saw this coming started to surface. Together we learned, and little by little the possibility that learning could continue in nontraditional ways became reality.

The same reality occurred months later when schools were faced with how to honor students for four years of hard work when most of the world was still shut down. Holding a high school graduation ceremony seemed to be an impossible feat until it wasn't. Virtual graduation, drive-by celebratory ceremonies, graduation car parades, and even parking lots filled with graduates honking for each other as principals called their names from loudspeakers commenced.

Once again, people came together and started to see what would stick when what they always knew and relied on was no longer an option. Throwing spaghetti with a little creativity doesn't hurt either.

That's the beauty of possibility. It's always present, even when you can't see it or you don't know what step to take to find it. That summer night in June, on a day that started like any other, John took me by the hand and my blue dress twirled into a new love that I didn't see coming. And neither did he.

Turned out two months later, he realized I was ready for a long-term commitment and he just wasn't there yet. I wanted to be mad. I thought

I'd walk away like I always did, feeling sorry for myself, feeling rejected, but instead I walked away feeling lucky that I had met someone like him. He was so honest and kind that I walked away respecting his thoughtful, mature decision to let me go. I didn't hate him and I didn't feel broken. I felt whole and grateful that I was strong enough to embrace love again. More importantly, I was okay alone and I wasn't willing to hold on when John said to let go.

What is for you will always be right on time. Never forget that. Missed buses. Doors closed. Events sold out. No more reservations. The college that didn't offer you a scholarship. The girl or guy who wasn't ready for a commitment. The house that sold to someone else. The prom that never happened because a worldwide pandemic hit. All of these events have one thing in common: they were not meant for you.

Okay, they have two things in common: they were not meant for you and they suck. The spaghetti that doesn't stick may feel like disappointment, but it leaves room for what is for you. It doesn't get in your way, and better yet, it doesn't waste your time. Embrace faith that you never miss anything while throwing spaghetti. It will stick when it's supposed to.

John taught me I was capable of being in and leaving a mature relationship. John taught me to be brave and reminded me that good, honest people still exist. Think of all you've gained from experiences on the path to finding what is for you. This includes relationships you've fostered and those you've left behind.

Although still single, I was happy and surrounded by belief that every day had potential. If you are not waking up in this mindset each day, highlight these words, or write them on a Post-it and stick it on your bathroom mirror or, better yet, make them your screensaver: **Every day has great potential.** Then smile knowing it's out there. *It* is different for each of us and *it* can and will change, but you have to trust *it's* coming.

In other words, spaghetti will never stick if you roll your eyes and go order yourself a pizza. I chose to spend my time being content, for the first time in a long time, with who I was and with people I loved including my married friends: Nikki and Tom, Krista and Tony, Brad and Raffaella, and Tara and Steve. I guess now's a good time to tell you I was in thirteen weddings. I know what you're thinking, *always a bridesmaid, never a bride.* Keep reading.

Before I continue, I just want to make a note about Tara and Steve. Yes, they had been together since the eighth grade, and, yes, the picture of them at the eighth-grade dinner dance next to their wedding photo makes a unique display in their living room. It is a foolproof conversation starter for all romantics. And, yes, their journey to the altar was sweet, innocent, and filled with love, but it was not without drama, breakups, and tears too.

I point this out to dispel the belief that high school sweethearts marry without bumps in the road. Or that any relationship grows without some growing pains. I think it's important to look behind the curtain of the class couple superlative because, growing up, this may be one myth you fantasize about. This along with the "you meet your husband in college" myth can be a tough pill to swallow when neither happen.

The reality is like—spoiler alert—finding out Santa Claus doesn't exist. Sure, you still have the potential to get presents and celebrate, but the magic is gone. What you may believe to be true just isn't and it's okay, it just takes time to adjust to whatever way your story goes. Remember, you won't miss a thing.

There I was, playing the role of the single girl, again. It didn't take long for Tara and the other girls to find a guy for me to date. "Date him for us," they said, as they gazed at an adorable guy across the room (we'll call him CJ). He caught my eye and we started to talk. The married girls were right. He was an Adonis; he was sweet and had a kind, baby face with beautiful eyes, and a killer body. We exchanged numbers, and just like that I was dating again.

CJ and I met for dinner a few nights later. We went to the movies. We met for coffee. We met out for drinks. He met some of my friends. I met his friends. I even joined him at a few Christmas parties that year. Although he was younger than I was, he wasn't afraid to talk about his long-term goals and about his desire to get married and have children. He checked all the boxes. I honestly couldn't find one thing wrong with him. Well, except, he wasn't John.

It wasn't fair for me to continue getting to know CJ when I knew he wasn't the one for me. Heartbreak had taught me that if he was right, I wouldn't be thinking about John. Because John didn't make me think about Tommy. That's what should happen when it's right. So, I knew CJ wasn't right. And, damn it, if John taught me anything, he taught me honesty. And, just like that, I let a perfectly eligible nice guy walk out of my life because I couldn't stop thinking about a guy who didn't think about me.

I wish my story was unique, but more often than not, the stars just don't align when it comes to love. You've probably read enough Shakespeare to know it really is an old tale: he loves her, she doesn't love him, and she loves a he that loves another she. Sometimes, he isn't even looking for a she. He's looking for a he. Bottom line: everyone is unsatisfied and miserable.

Dwelling in a place of unhappiness only perpetuates more misery. I'm sure you've heard some variation of this truth before, but the only way to truly understand and have faith in this truth is to test the opposite effect. The law of attraction suggests that we possess the power to focus on what we truly want and use our energy to pull into our lives our deepest desires. This philosophy sounds too good to be true, right?

Listen, it's okay to brush this law off as pseudoscience, but a change in thinking can create change. The simple idea that thoughts become things continues to prove to be true. I bet you've experienced your mind taking over and perpetuating an outcome.

"Ugh! I have a physics test next period. I'm totally going to fail. It's going to be impossible. The smartest kid in the class is probably going to fail. Why should I even bother taking it?" Fast-forward to a week later. You earned yourself a lovely 56 percent, just as you predicted.

So why not use your thinking for good? Can't hurt. Bet it helps.

Most of us are raised to be on the defensive and to worry about what could go wrong and to do our best to be ready for it. Living this way creates a major block for whatever you desire to flow easily into your life. What took me years to figure out became crystal clear as a twelfth grader stood up in front of her classmates to read a personal essay. She shared that she suffered a stroke when she was two years old.

While she did recover and was fortunate to live a stable, healthy life for the next three years, at five years old she began to have brain seizures that resulted in the removal of the left side of her brain. She was forced to live in a hospital for nearly seven months. Clearly this took a toll on her mental health. She shared difficult memories of feeling sad and refusing to speak.

Her classmates listened in respectful silence as she declared the important words she clung to as she fought for her physical and mental health: "This disability was not going to be a setback, it was going to be my superpower." She believed maintaining a positive mindset was the only option if she wanted to get well and find her way out of the hospital. As a child, she was blessed to see this philosophy prove its truth and vowed to live her life seeing what could go right.

As she faced another health challenge during her junior year of high school, her ability to walk was at stake. She felt the fear and worry creep up through her veins. She wrestled with the possibility that she would be stuck in a wheelchair forever. Questions of what if and how surfaced and once again she relied on her ability to think positively. Her unwavering faith in the power of her own mindset faced another surgery and another recovery. She tests the power of positive thinking each day, as she lives her life with unique challenges, and still continues to be a light.

Misery loves company. So be bad company for those who dwell in the negative and can't see their way out of it. Ignoring the worry and possible negative outcomes as you live boldly as if all your desires are in reach can be scary and may be uncomfortable at first. But imagine how you could benefit from seeing your best self each day and trusting that your life holds great potential. With gratitude for all you have accomplished, and what you have to offer, you can live your life joyfully right this moment. Understanding this principle can help you move through life with conviction and confidence.

With a tornado in my belly, and a cleansing breath, I reached deep down to the bottom of that boiling pot of spaghetti and threw one last piece at the wall. It didn't matter that it had been over a year since I spoke to John. I was ready for what I somehow knew was for me. I dialed John's number and left an unscripted, authentically me message.

It went something like this: *Hi, John, it's Melissa. You're probably wondering why I'm calling you, and honestly I can't believe I'm calling you either, but I just wanted to see how you were doing and, um, I don't know. I missed you. Okay. Give me a call. Bye.*

I hung up and just knew that was it. It was our time. Hours later, my cell phone rang in the living room just as I was about to jump in the shower. As I listened to the ringing, a sense of calmness came over my whole body. I didn't need to run across my condo to answer it. I didn't need to watch the phone to see if he called. I didn't need to do anything. Everything I ever wanted was mine. I just knew it. I trusted myself and I trusted that John knew it too.

He often tells me not to tell this story because he doesn't think it's common. He believes that most guys end relationships because the relationship

isn't right, not because the timing is off. He worries that our story could give a vulnerable person
false hope. This may be true. And, sure, moving on
is important, and leaving relationships that aren't
mutual is important, but so is trusting your heart
and moving confidently toward what you know is
meant for you. You'll know the difference; you just
have to listen to your heart and throw spaghetti,
with no regrets.

Objective: Live Happily Ever After?

S hortly after John and I were married, I was browsing around one of those dollar stores where really nothing is actually a dollar. You know those stores where there is a bunch of stuff you really don't need, but somehow your mind tricks you into thinking you are getting a great deal because you are in a self-proclaimed bargain store. The items typically have orange stickers announcing prices that actually, if you cared to do the research, are well above the worth of the piece of shit you don't really need anyway.

I do love these stores and find it easy to get lost in these places. I rarely leave with nothing. I attribute these needless purchases to my grandma Lilla who also still loves these stores. As a child, I would walk in John's Bargain Store in the Bronx and she would say, "You can have anything you want." This idea appealed to me even then as it appeals to most of us now, well, until we learn that this may not always be true.

It was in one of these overpriced dollar stores that I discovered the sign that now hangs on the wall in the house John and I live in with our three children. If I remember correctly, I bought it at a store called Just a Buck, which in retrospect should have been called a Bunch of Bucks, because that is what I actually paid. Nevertheless, the sign reads: And, They Lived Happily Ever After.

I bought this sign because, to me, it was whimsical and romantic and the perfect way to describe what the future held. We were young, although older than most married couples starting out, and we had the promise of building a house together and having children. We were both established in our careers, so there was nothing holding us back from running full speed into the happily ever after that we imagined.

The key word here is *imagined*. Imagine by definition, according to *Merriam-Webster*, is a form of mental image of something not present. I have spent a significant part of my life imagining. I imagined what college felt like, what type of teacher I would be, how married life would look, the kind of mom I would be, and I even imagined what it would feel like to finish this book and see it in your hands. Imagining can be one of our greatest tools as we look to prioritize what is most important in our lives.

I wholeheartedly believe in the power of a vision board. However, it's important to note that, by definition, imagining is to envision mental images of what is not present. While I encourage you to imagine all that you want for yourself, I think it's important to stop, be present, and perhaps drop the *ever after* and simply live happily. Believe it or not, this state of mind is your compass and will help determine where you go next. I'm not saying not to imagine all that you hope to possess, or aspire to be, but I am saying that what you need to be happy is in your reach right now even if now does not match your imagination.

When you're single, around the holidays, it's easy to lament over the fact that you're missing out on spending fall fun and holidays with someone special. Imagine a bunch of sorority girls sitting around during this special time of year, some single, some with partners. It's easy for fantasies to emerge: a walk through the pumpkin patch, complete with a stunning background of foliage, with a significant other; an impromptu ice-skating date at the local pond where you hold hands as you teach each other how to glide on the ice; a frolic in the soft snow, perhaps ending in a snowball fight and a chilly embrace; or a sweet, unexpected kiss under the mistletoe. These are images that make it into every Hallmark movie, rom-com, and teen drama. Of course these tropes become part of our fantasy land. How could they not?

My friend Nicole listened to this nonsense, as girls expressed their longing for this type of love, and blatantly said, "Really? I've been with my boyfriend since we were eighteen, and we never once did any of this!" After a good laugh, we had no choice but to examine the difference between imagination and reality. I, too, had been in relationships that never led me to a pumpkin patch or to ice skating around the Christmas tree at Rockefeller Center, or to any of these other Hollywood moments.

I also imagined being a mom would be way easier than it actually is. I would huff in frustration at moms who would block the hallways in the mall with their obnoxious strollers on Black Friday when I just wanted to get to my favorite stores to catch the best deals. Well that is until I became one of these annoying moms and had no choice but to literally stroll through the mall if I even could get there at all. Insert eye roll emoji here.

These are just two of the many times my imagination led me down a tunnel of truth that didn't even exist. Let me tell you, it's not easy to climb out of an imaginary tunnel that is filled with false, yet appealing, images. It takes time to look around and wonder where all those daydreams went.

It's kind of like that outfit you see online and suddenly you just have to have it because your favorite influencer looks super cute, offered a code, and linked all the items. You easily picture yourself adorned head to toe in the OOTD you see online. It's a no brainer. You're like Ariana Grande in 2019. You want it. You got it.

You know exactly where you will wear it and can't wait to show it off. You even pulled out a few accessories you think will be perfect additions to the look. And then it shows up at your door. You can't wait to try it on, you have yourself convinced it's going to be perfect. Until you actually try it on. *What the hell?* You think to yourself, as you look in the mirror. *Is this the same outfit I fell in love with online?* You adjust your top to see if you can make it work. You grab a pair of shoes, because they might help. You even pull up the picture you loved to compare the looks. You were so sure this outfit was going to be adorable on you. Alas you realize what a pain it's going to be to mail it all back. Damn. Your imagination got ya again. How did that happen?

Find Your Reality

Senior year is the time when our imaginations really take off. We imagine what our next chapters will be, and, typically, these next steps are attached to the colleges that somewhere along the line you or someone in your family or at school mentioned would be a good fit for you and within your reach in terms of your academic record.

As a teacher of seniors, here's what I have seen play out countless times: September is filled with excitement of finally being at the top of the academic food chain. Finally, this new senior class comes in with the courses they are excited to take, the schedule that allows for free time, and many times, these kids even get their own parking spots. Then I mention the college essay, and guidance counselors match students up on college application databases that will store all of their information, so actually applying to schools will be a few quick clicks away.

This start of the college process is where senior year goes from exciting to terrifying for most students. While imagining senior year as freshmen, thoughts of parties, senior trips, and the prom were well thought out, but the reality of facing the grades earned along the way and filling out college applications were not so much a part of the daydreams. I've actually heard kids say, "I wish I could do high school over," when they look at grades that could have been better and application building opportunities that were missed.

Regardless, as the end of October rolls around, college essays are finalized and college visits are well underway and the process continues. By the time we hit January, most kids are relieved that their applications are sent and they can finally sit back and play the waiting game.

Unfortunately, here's what often happens during the waiting game. Imagination kicks in, and, suddenly, ideas of campus life on college X or being at college Y with their best friend or living in the dorm they saw at college Z becomes part of the story they begin to tell and hold on to. Imagining life after high school begins to happen and the vision begins to take real shape and it begins to feel comfortable and familiar. This is what we all do when faced with change.

By the time colleges start responding, most kids know deep down where they want to wind up if at all. This raises the stakes they didn't initially know were so high. *Damn you, sophomore math class! I wish I had joined more clubs in high school. Ugh! I should have never quit the scouts. That teacher never liked me, why did I take her class?* Suddenly, worry, regret, fear, and tremendous hope are all rolled up in those applications sent out into the world and there is nothing left to do but wait.

If you ever waited for anything, you know that seconds feel like minutes, minutes feel like hours, and days feel like weeks. Some of these schools will even put you on a waitlist or just wait until May to reveal their final decisions. It's not easy, to say the least, and the process can create a dense cumulonimbus cloud around your senior year. If you don't know what a cumulonimbus cloud is, *damn*. You should have paid more attention in science too.

College rejection can be a difficult pill to swallow. The sooner you are able to turn *no* into the right *yes* for you, the better off you are going to be. This is not only true for the college rejection, it's true for all the other times your imagination screws you over. Your imagination will paint some unbelievable stuff, but don't let it throw you for a loop when what you imagined doesn't unfold like a pop-up picture book before your eyes. Instead, keep turning the pages until you find your reality.

The college of your dreams will not reject you. If the college rejects you, it is not the college for you. The right school will not leave you feeling inadequate or like a failure. It will root for you and help you find a way to succeed as you propel into your next big thing. And, although this is not based on any scientific research, I've seen this scenario play out so many times it's boring.

If you choose, you will go to a college that accepts you and you will return home to report that you love it. And if you don't, who cares? Just pick up your years' worth of college credits and consider a transfer or stay home. Ultimately, you get to do whatever you want except get stuck in what you imagined and hide from what you are actually facing. Accepting change is part of living happily. The sooner you learn this simple fact, the better you will be.

I used to fight against the tide. I would find myself frustrated when things just didn't play out the way I wanted them to. To be honest, this was often a source of my unhappiness. I would find myself stuck in the way I thought it was supposed to be instead of seeing the grace in what was right in front of me. Another classic case of if I knew then what I know now. Pictures of me in college reveal a thinner, younger, brighter version of me. At the time, I thought I was fat. Damn it. I wasn't fat. I was just stuck in a narrative of what skinny looked like and completely missed that I was already there.

I cried the entire day before I got married. Sobbed getting my hair washed and dried, cried getting my nails done, all because the threat of a major snowstorm was on the horizon. I completely missed the joy that was supposed to lead up to my wedding day. Sure. It was a blizzard the day we said I do, but I married a guy who cracks me up, loves me, and has a pure heart.

It's easy to feel sorry for yourself when life kicks you in the ass. It's important to recognize when you are slipping down to a woe-is-me space and you start to hear imaginary violins playing. Bryan, a student in my class recently admitted he was falling into this space. He fell into a pattern of skipping school, missing assignments, and believing that if only his family was whole, he'd have the life he really wanted and deserved. As consequences for his behavior started to catch up with him, he had no choice but to reevaluate his behavior.

He recognized that he was feeling sorry for himself and finally got to a place where he knew it was time to face mistakes that led him to feelings of failure and disappointment. He started by changing his daily habits. This included going to the gym to improve his self-esteem and making connections with positive people. Attending school and staying on top of his classwork became a priority again. He also enlisted the help of his teachers and started to communicate when he needed support.

The greatest change came when Bryan learned to stop blaming external elements, specifically the instability around his upbringing, and instead took responsibility for his actions and the way he carried himself. He assessed his present and stopped blaming his past, and most importantly he didn't doom his future. He accepted where his life led him and found appreciation for the experiences that challenged him and helped him grow closer to his true self. What a gift that he learned the benefit and joy that is laced in life's ups and downs.

I can probably tell you a million other examples, but I know I can't stop you from trying to catch your expectations. I wish I could teach you to appreciate the moments that are happening in your senior year that you may be missing because your imagination thought it was supposed to look some other way or because unforeseen circumstances you can't control have come into play.

How Can You Find Happiness Every Day?

What action can you take today? I would be remiss if I didn't pause right here to mention how practicing gratitude can change your life. If you've never tried this daily practice, this is one easy routine you can start today. It just might surprise you how something so simple can create massive change.

I present this concept to my seniors as I assign them to write gratitude letters. They write to people they are thankful for as they get ready to graduate. Then, after writing and revising their letters, they call whoever they wrote to and read their letter to them.

Imagine calling your mom, dad, grandparent, best friend, or whoever else has held your hand through life and surprising them with words too often unsaid. Sweet sentiments like, "Dad, Thanks for offering me desserts at restaurants . . . thanks for teaching me discipline and respect," are expressed sometimes for the first time during this assignment.

A few students even bring teachers to tears as they are called out of class to listen to letters of gratitude from former students. Nothing is more rewarding to your teacher than hearing things like, "Thank you for believing in me," or "You inspired me to pursue my dream."

Making these calls or sharing these letters face-to-face and acknowledging the benefits of expressing gratitude is an experiment I learned to conduct from watching *Soul Pancake: The Science of Happiness*. It works every time. My students finish sharing letters and often come back to class smiling or misty-eyed because of the beautiful exchange they encountered with someone they love. They agree—gratitude is powerful and uplifting. They promise to practice this more often and then, poof, the bell rings and the magic is gone.

I can't blame them. I didn't know any of this in high school or even college. Sure, Oprah said something about a gratitude journal, but she was a middle-aged woman and a billionaire. What did I have in common with her? Not much, but I sure as hell was going to try what she was doing. Clearly, it was working.

What do you have in common with me? I know, high school. And I know everyone sits in the same seat. We just choose to get up and go different places. Go with gratitude and you will see beautiful moments you never expected.

Life is not a highlight reel, TikTok video, social media picture dump, or a filtered Instagram post. But it will bring you buzzer-beater moments if you let it. I've watched all of my nieces and nephews play sports, and I've seen them take incredible shots, win games they weren't supposed to win, and block goals that should have gone in. Sitting in stands, on benches, on sidelines, in gyms, I've had the joy of watching kids revel in true buzzer-beater moments. You know, the moment when the clock sounds and the shot remains en route to its target. This is the buzzer-beater moment. When the basket counts, the crowd goes wild, and that kid who took the shot becomes a small town hero for a moment in time and lives a story that will be told well beyond adolescence.

This type of moment is my wish for all of you. These moments do not look the same for all of us. If you are waiting for your moment to look like someone else's, you may very well miss your moment.

Earning a standing ovation as you finish singing "The Winner Takes It All" as the lead role in your school's version of *Mamma Mia* may be your moment. Perhaps standing by the body of artwork you've created for the spring art show accepting compliments and answering questions is your moment. Organizing a poetry slam and watching your peers show up may be your moment. Dancing at the prom as you celebrate four years with the kids you've come to love may be your moment. Perhaps your moment is finally receiving that college acceptance letter.

I've seen three soccer teams win state championships. I've seen a football team win a state championship and its players and coaches return to school as local heroes. I've seen that same team tragically lose its football coach two short seasons later and raise over $65,000 to make sure his son wouldn't have to face financial struggle. Although vastly different, these are all moments of great triumph. Sometimes these moments rise after defeat.

You see, these are the moments that you don't forget. These are the moments when reality exceeds imagination, and *ever after* doesn't matter. These are the moments I wish for you. Moments of simply living happily in the here and now.

Objective: Graduate with Grace

They shared the weight of memory. They took up what others could no longer bear. Often, they carried each other, the wounded or weak. They carried infections. They carried chess sets, basket-balls, Vietnamese-English dictionaries, insignia of rank, Bronze Stars and Purple Hearts, plastic cards imprinted with the Code of Conduct. They carried diseases, among them malaria and dysentery. They carried lice and ringworm and leeches and paddy algae and various rots and molds. They carried the land itself—Vietnam, the place, the soil—a pow-dery orange-red dust that covered their boots and fatigues and faces. They carried the sky.

This is an excerpt from the book *The Things They Carried,* where Tim O'Brien discusses what soldiers may have carried during and after the Vietnam War. The first line acknowledges these brave young men and their shared experience of facing the horrors of war.

Look around. Who will live in your memory and be part of your story? Who helped you carry the sky, especially in those times when growing up felt too heavy to bear alone?

Tim O'Brien's book is the first book I ever taught to high school seniors. As most of my students know, his book is one of my absolute favorites, not only because the writing is flawless, but because it reminds me to consider what I have spent my career carrying.

Turns out, I've been carrying this book (the one you are reading right now) in the depths of my soul. Actually, this is the sixth book I've been holding in my heart. Four of these earlier manuscripts were picture books. The first one I wrote was inspired by the passing of my first and only dog, Buddy. The second was all about kids at the lunch table eating healthy and unhealthy snacks, and that night one little boy dreams he becomes a French fry. It was a silly little book I adored because, well, I love French fries just like the main character.

As my writing matured and I began to dive into the world of picture books more deeply, I was inspired to write *Girls Who Glitter,* a story of a girl who was *that* girl in school that all the other little girls wanted to be. The story reveals how girls do not need to compete; they can simply shine brighter and sparkle with joy together.

Finally, I wrote a picture book inspired by my three boys. I hope to see this in full color one day. The funny thing is I wouldn't even care if anyone bought the book; some things we just do because they matter to us. I imagine my boys reading this book to their own kids someday and saying, "Grandma wrote this." Holy shit. That thought is a little too scary, maybe I'll hold off on this publication.

Before writing these books, I struggled for years to complete a young adult novel I started while doing my Master of Fine Arts in Writing. Consequently, I never finished it because part of the main conflict did not add up. For years, I would pick up my manuscript and try to force sense onto its pages. When I thought about this unfinished manuscript, feelings of failure slithered up and coiled around my heart like a boa constrictor; I felt like a failure. I am an English teacher. I preach day in and day out that the only way to be successful is to work. Then periodically, I would stumble across this manuscript and become overwhelmed with disappointment and regret. I always dreamed of being a writer. Yet, day by day my goal slipped away for one reason only: I was not working on it.

After my third son turned eight months old, I decided I could no longer motivate my students without also pushing myself. I refused to look back at my career and feel like a fraud. I went back to work on writing picture books, creating new characters, and focusing on my forever goal of becoming a published author. I started talking to my friends and to my students about what I wanted to accomplish. And time and time again, I would get comments like, *I can't wait to read your book, I bet it is hysterical.* Or people would ask, *Did you write about me?*

For a while, I ignored these comments and laughed off these questions and stayed the course. Truth be told, my picture books weren't really funny, and I certainly wasn't writing about the people in my life. It is no surprise that none of these books found their way out of my computer and onto any bookshelf.

Go for It

Then on the third day of 2019, lying next to my second son who was struggling to fall asleep, I pulled out my phone. The screen lit up a small space in his room and under Notes I started to type with my thumbs. My son drifted off to sleep as I drafted the first chapter of this book. Later that night I found myself typing furiously on my computer. I have never written so fast and with such intention and ease.

I just started writing what I knew about most: my life, being a teacher, and hanging out with teenagers. As I wrote, and each word found its way onto the pages of this book, I started to let go of the fear that I was teaching what I was too scared to do for myself. I welcomed fear. I was going for it.

I started writing this book. Inspired by each of you. You, my actual students, and you, my students who opened this book and hopefully don't feel so alone in this unsettling stage of adolescence. This is the book I was meant to write and I was meant to share. I have been carrying the weight of this book. What relief and joy it is to put these pages in your capable hands.

Some of these stories I have told over the years. Some of these stories I wish I had time to tell or I was brave enough to reveal sooner. These are the stories I wish my high school teacher had told me. It's also filled with all I have learned from each of you. Before I go, thank you to all of you who have passed through my classroom, room 207, or who have turned the pages of this book. Believe me. Without you, I couldn't have written a word.

And now, as it is almost time for us to part ways, and I am about to let this book go, I ask you to take a moment and think about what you are carrying. Is it a dream? A fear? A painful past? Or perhaps it is a longing for someone or something? Maybe you are carrying guilt. Or pride. Are you carrying anger or regret? Are you carrying satisfaction?

Once you become aware of those intangibles, ask yourself this: Is what you are carrying worth hanging onto or is it weighing you down, or worse holding you back from grabbing something that would otherwise be within your reach? Think about it, because when you carry something others can't see, only you can put it down.

Consider this: If you know you are carrying something around, what makes you think the person sitting next to you doesn't have a few life experiences that he or she is carrying around? This may be a wonderful gift, it may also explain why people behave the way they do. Maybe the hot kid with the killer smile who acts like a jerk or the nasty girl with the perfect body who thinks she is better than everyone else is much, much more than what you think you see. Cut people some slack. For maybe, just maybe they can't let go of that thing weighing them down. Be sympathetic instead of angry, or mean. Inevitably, it will make your load lighter.

As a teacher, it is my nature to ask questions. As an English teacher, I tend to ask many questions that never end in a definite answer. For those of you who love math and take comfort in 2+2 equaling 4, this type of inquiry just may be your worst nightmare. But how else can you approach the art of understanding the other guy if you are not willing to consider the various sides of the same story?

You see, I've learned that although we may all be in the same place at the same time, our experience in that moment is often vastly different. Take a Friday night game under the lights. Many, many people gather in the same place and see the same game. But the losing team has a completely different version of the play-by-play than the winning team.

This is life. We are all here, but how we receive each moment is based on everything we've lived and all we carry with us. It's taken me a long time to realize this. But I often wonder about the world around me and make every attempt possible to consider what the other guy may be feeling. As a teacher, sometimes I get it. Sometimes I miss.

When I first started teaching, I couldn't wait to inspire the sea of diverse teenagers that I was blessed to teach. Naively, I thought that I could make every one of my students love writing just like I do. So that first awkward year, in my tenth-grade classes, I integrated daily journal writing and hoped they would experience the pure joy of the written word. I would post writing prompts on the board every day. The prompts would be anything from *write about what you did this weekend* to *where do you hope to be in ten years.* I couldn't wait to collect these journals at the end of the week. I imagined the pages to be filled with positive, fun, thoughtful responses. My high school self would have loved these daily assignments. However, I didn't always get what I was hoping for from my students.

One September, I assigned the following journal topic: *Write about a significant event and discuss how that event changed and/or shaped the person you are today.* Here's what one student turned in:

I am hurt. I am angry. I feel pain. I feel remorse. I struggle. Tragedy inflicted all these feelings within my heart, mind and soul. I lost my cousin Cello. My world yet to exist just a kid only eleven and destiny struck hard. I've been shaped with sharp corners. I am strong. I am solid. I am smart. I understand. I build; I am divine due to the episodes of my life after this event. I had to maintain and be strong in order to survive. I had to born knowledge and accept my past. The event I witnessed was the eight story fall that sent my cousin to the gates of heaven.

And then, on the bottom line of his journal entry, this young student wrote a note to me. It said, *Be careful with questions you ask, you just might get real answers.*

I've kept his journal for the length of my career because I never wanted to forget this student's tragic, yet poetic words. Here's what it taught me and here is my advice to you. Don't be afraid to ask questions. If someone lets you in and offers an unexpected response, consider yourself lucky. Because without strong human connections, you will miss out on the best of what this life has to offer.

Ask questions because an answer, any answer, may ignite a new perspective. Awareness is a gift. The simple recognition of universality can get you far.

It Ain't Over Till It's Over

Over the years, I have heard many of you say that soon you must face the "real world." I hope you now realize, without question, that you're already here. In fact, you've been here for quite some time. This is the real world. You leave impressions, you matter, and you are already making a difference to me, your parents, your friends, and you will impact all the people who haven't even met you yet. Be proud of the impression you leave as you move through this life.

Be kind to yourself. Stop comparing yourself to the people around you or, worse, stop imagining the life that may or may not be the reality attached to the pictures you see on social media. Yes, those pictures tell stories, but I promise they hide so much more. Stop comparing yourself to someone's end game. Remember that anyone who appears to be who you aspire to be has made many, many mistakes. Take the time to really know people and appreciate their stories. Don't forget the people you already know and cherish the time, advice, and relationships you have already been fortunate to receive from others.

Finally, please remember: "It ain't over till it's over" and although this may not be the grammatically correct advice you were hoping for as we say goodbye, it's the truth. If you don't get everything you need or want immediately, don't stop reaching for it. You will be successful, but only if you don't give up on yourself. Gain momentum. Look at your track record and celebrate your wins. Better yet, use them as fuel to take the next step on your way to the top. Not everyone does their homework, not everyone passes the test, not everyone passes the class, not everyone graduates. So when you see your list of accomplishments, don't dismiss your wins. Not everyone can do what you can.

I used to tell my students to dream big and then multiply the size of that dream by a thousand. But in the words of Shonda Rhimes, "Ditch the dream and be a doer." Because sometimes the dream isn't half of what you can really do.

I declared I would never be a teacher. I had no idea what this side of the desk looked like. I had no idea that this career would lead me here. But I kept pushing myself and letting my heart lead. I suggest you do the same. Because, somehow, you will wind up exactly where you are meant to be. Here I am sharing my stories and fulfilling my childhood dream of writing a book I had no idea was inside of me.

Thank you for coming on this journey with me. It's been a pleasure sharing these moments with each of you. What a gift to spend time with great people I have never met before and reconnect with students I haven't seen since your last bell rang.

Whoever you are, no matter why you are here, you are on the precipice of something amazing. Because, something great is always waiting for you. Please. Do not be afraid to run in the direction of your dreams and embrace them as they shift and change and take new shape to help you create the beautiful life you are meant to live. A life where you, my friend, live in the left lane.

Put your blinker on, shift gears, and wave to your competition as you take off. I hope your car is filled with love and passion for what makes you truly happy. Only you have the power to hit the gas, so go. Go. Go. Seriously, stop reading and go get what's meant for you. I hope our time together served you well. Thanks for hanging out beyond the bell.

A Note to Parents

My first instinct when sitting down to write this is to simply say: back off. But, like most of the chapters in this book, my students have shared so many important notes that I have no choice but elaborate and explain this sentiment based on all I've learned about your kids. This chapter is for all the parents who have struggled to stay connected to their teenage child during the long, winding, sometimes painful years of adolescence. While the underlying current of this chapter will be to back off, I will give you a little more to chew on.

Quick disclaimer: Your kids told me this. Don't hold what you are about to read against me. Thank me. In fact, you're welcome. I'm letting you into a sacred space that your teenagers and I share. However, I am not breaking their trust. It's quite the contrary; in fact, let's just say your kids and I have a mutual understanding and it's this: you need a talking to.

Let me start off by saying I have three kids. I get it. This is tough stuff. When I first started teaching, I was young, single, and harsh with my students. I accepted few excuses and drew a hard line. People said things like *when you have kids you will understand*, and *you'll be a better teacher when you have kids of your own*. I hated these comments. No, I didn't hate them, I loathed them. Simply because I took extreme offense to these suggestions that because I wasn't a parent, I was less of a teacher than someone with kids. It felt like these comments suggested that I had no idea how to handle my students in my classroom. That just didn't sit well with me. And then I had kids.

Damn. It's not that I wasn't a good teacher before, and it's not that being tough and holding kids accountable is wrong, it's just that high school kids are kids. Correction. High school kids are your kids. And before I had my own kids, I didn't see them as newborn babies that kept you up at night, toddlers that smiled and played on the monkey bars, or young learners heading off on the first day of school.

I had no reference to the visual of your kid sitting on a school bus, barely tall enough to see out of the window to frantically wave goodbye, as the bus pulled away from the safety of your embrace. I didn't see how sweet it was to see your child running toward you with fists full of dandelions picked just for you. I just saw my students in the moment that I met them, in my classroom, for that year I had to teach them. I always believed my job was simply to prepare them for what came next. I was so focused on preparing them for their college years that *the before* didn't really matter to me until I had kids.

Therefore, although I can't stand it because, seriously, who really likes being wrong? It is true: being a parent has made me a better teacher.

I now understand completely how that one kid in my room who is one of thousands I've taught is your entire world. And his or her experience in my room is all you care about. I also know that while I grade stacks of papers each time I hand out an assignment, all you care about is the one paper with the one grade that is on your kid's record.

Because that record will be just that, a record that will never disappear. Right now, it matters. It matters so much that you can hardly sleep some nights. It matters so much that you sometimes lose sight of your own teenager because when you communicate, that record hangs between you.

Although I am not a therapist, and do not have any degree that certifies me as an expert in family therapy, what I do have is years of logged hours. I have spent half of my life with your kids. I do feel well qualified to ask you to consider an extremely important question: what the hell are you doing?

I know it's been a long time since you were in high school, so your memory most likely does not serve you well here. And, yes, I'm asking you to trust me. Essentially, it's like I never graduated from high school, so it's clear to me that kids today are no different from the way you were in high school, than we were in high school. The music, hairstyles, clothing, and technology have all changed, but many things are still the same.

Like you, your kids are dying for acceptance. Like you, your kids are trying to balance school, friends, relationships, and extracurricular activities. Like you, your kids do not want their parents on their backs. Like you did with your parents, after a while, your kids stopped listening to you.

This is the hard truth. Just like it was the truth for you. Kids haven't changed. Just because you are now the parent doesn't mean that your kid will find you any less annoying than you found your parents to be when you were in high school.

If you're reading this thinking you were not as challenging as your own teenager, think about all the crazy stuff you did that your parents knew nothing about. I bet there are even a few secrets they still don't know about your high school years. Cut your kid some slack. You have more in common than you think.

If your memory painted a different picture of your adolescence filled with positivity, hard work, perfect grades, and respect for elders, that may all be true, but what have you blocked out? Think about it: Do you remember your test grades in biology? Do you remember how many missing homework assignments you had in math? What about the time you clocked when your phys ed teacher asked you to run the mile? How many times were you late for class? I am a high school teacher. I am an English teacher, and I can't remember most of the grades I earned in my English classes.

These specifics are probably not so clear for you either. And now I bet these specifics don't really matter or define who you have become.

Think about that the next time your kid comes home with a quiz he didn't study for or missed a homework assignment he blew off because it was his birthday weekend. Can you understand? Don't you have off days too? Are there some things that you can let go of with your own kid? Wouldn't it have been nice if your parents and teachers gave you a break once in a while?

The key is to be understanding within reason. I know this is a delicate dance, and I also know this is easier said than done. But if you don't want to be shut out, allow your kid to feel safe letting you in. Your kid needs that. Although you may be able to pull from your memory and relate to some of what your kid is going through, some of what your kid is experiencing is just harder.

The Stress of High School Is Real

Sure. The stress that comes with adolescence was real for you, too, but when the school day ended, when that bell rang, it was over. With the integration of technology, teachers (not this teacher of course) have the ability to assign, discuss, and require work be completed even when school ends. It's like the expectation of students now is that of a CEO with a company car and two cell phones.

Essentially, they can run, but they can't hide. Kids can't even cut a class these days without at least two different apps blowing the whistle on them. Some kids need this, they really do, and many times it can help, but don't be misled. I repeat, the stress of high school is real.

Try to be cool. However, you are not your kid's friend. I repeat, you are not your kid's friend. No one wants the parent who tries to hang with the teenagers. Most kids are successful because they have the support they need from the people who love them, not because their parents allow them to drink with their friends in their houses or throw pre-prom parties. Draw the line and be prepared to move it as your kid grows.

If missing homework assignments, weak quiz grades, failing tests, or below average essay grades becomes a pattern, it is your job to drop the hammer. Hold your kid accountable by letting him know he's better than the grades he's bringing home. Support him by letting him know that you believe in him and you believe in him because you've seen his track record. Give him the confidence to succeed because you've seen him do it many, many times.

Let your kid know, learning is a gift. Model respect for reading and hard work, get your head out of your phone, and watch how quickly your kid follows. It's always amazing when parents complain about the time their kids spend on social media or playing Xbox. Often, these are the same adults who pay the bills, buy the devices, and set no limits of their own. It's simple: monkey see, monkey do. Just because your baby is now in high school, doesn't mean she's too old for your attention. Give it to her now. Give her the positive attention you gave her when she started to talk. Remember how you cheered when she started to smack her lips together and say ma-ma? You smiled wide and cheered. That's all she needed then to keep trying, and it's probably all she needs now. That's all any of us need: the people we love to encourage us and stay close to us as we try and fail and try again.

Because my students don't always understand that most of your intentions are shining right at their best interests, they need you to let them figure it out sometimes. While we spend hours of free time coaching Little League teams, making cupcakes, chaperoning school trips, and hosting PTA meetings, sometimes our kids just want some space. Space is good. Kids don't need to fill every moment of their days with homework, after-school activities, sports, and work. Like adults, kids need down time. Your kid is exhausted. There is value in lying on the bed listening to music and being alone.

Before you insist, and convince yourself that everything you do has always been for your kid, be honest. Did you do these things for your kid or for yourself?

Which brings me to the most important part of this chapter. If you've tuned out or started skimming because all of this unsolicited advice is making you uncomfortable, I'm begging you, on your child's behalf, give this section your undivided attention. I know you can handle this, so listen up. As your child prepares for life after high school, please remember: You had your chance. Let your kid have his. I have had the same talk with my students so many times over the years that I can't believe parents haven't figured it out by now. But here it is one more time. I can't believe it took me this long to put this in writing.

Post–high school planning is daunting. It's difficult for you and for your kids. There are so many unknowns and so much build up to this moment that when it's finally here, everyone loses sight of what is truly important. I always ask my students during this process, and especially during the decision-making process, what's your end game? The answer to this question should drive every part of this stage and help clarify the final decision. Unfortunately, the path in this process is often muddy.

What school is Mark applying to? Simple question. Yet, I've seen parents clam up, stammer over words, giggle nervously, and blurt out lies. Why? Because somewhere between having kids, raising teenagers, and filling out college applications, parents began to take complete ownership over the response to this question as if the answer defined the last seventeen years of their parenting skills. High-priced school, great reputation, Ivy league = A+ parent. State school, merit money = B+ parent. Community college, two-year school, trade school = C+ parent. When this is spelled out, I'm sure you would quickly defend, deny, and explain that this type of judgment is something you just wouldn't do or have not experienced. However, can you honestly say you haven't judged, eye rolled, or felt jealous or frustrated by the pressure surrounding the college process?

How about we celebrate the fact that all post-secondary plans are exceptional? Parents, you are putting some of this pressure on each other. Step back. Remember we are all doing our best. That's the same for all of us regardless of the school our kids decide to attend or not. The decision of what to do after high school is their decision. Not yours.

It's Their Turn

Of course you want to give your kids the opportunity that you didn't get. Maybe you wish you had the chance to go to school. Perhaps you still spend time lamenting at work about what could have been, if only. I'm sure it must be difficult to worry and live in this regret. And I really am sorry for you and your missed opportunity, but you don't get to put your dream on your kid. It doesn't work. Unless of course you want your kid to resent you. Let your kid find his or her own path. In order for this to happen, you need to trust your own parenting. You've offered what you can, now it's their turn to make hard decisions.

Choosing a college and choosing a major is not like choosing what to eat for dinner. Sure, it would be great if your kids ate lean chicken, vegetables, a big green salad, a small portion of rice, and drank water each night to create a perfect balance of all food groups. Guess what? Your kid probably wants pizza and pizza will be just fine. They won't go hungry. Get it? Your suggestions are welcome I'm sure, but, ultimately, kids needs to live out the choices they make. After all, do you want to be the reason your student is two years into a degree in engineering only to discover it wasn't what he wanted to pursue in the first place? Or worse, do you want your kid to hate college or drop out because your choice wasn't the right fit?

Like adults, high school kids seek approval from the people they love: their friends, teachers, siblings, and most of all you. It is not unlikely that they will pursue a path after high school that they know will make you happy because this is a huge decision, and they feel the weight of it just like you do. Help them make the best decision, but let them lead on this one. It's their turn, don't take it from them.

Most of us wind up doing what our parents told us to on our first go-around as professionals. Let your kid fast-forward through this and help them pursue their passion and live out the life that you prepared them for. And now as we part ways, I leave you with this: it's time to have faith in your kid, have faith in the job you've done and just do what you've always done—hope for the best and love unconditionally.

Acknowledgments

First and foremost, to all my students who passed through room 207, you will always be "my kids." Thanks for teaching me how to teach what matters most.

Special thanks to the class of 2019, especially Sammi Reyes. Thank you all for handling me with care after I had my third son and motivating me to write this book. We dreamed big together.

Patti DeMatteo, thank you for believing in this book and my ability to teach outside the walls of that amazing high school in Westchester County.

My colleagues and dear friends, especially Allison Ferrier and Carol Lieto, who read this book when it was in its first stage and cheered me on every step of the way.

Everyone at G&D Media, thank you for taking a chance on this labor of love. You just may be the kindest, most patient publishers in the business.

My editor Sandra Wendel who taught this English teacher more than a thing or two about writing. I am forever grateful for your care and kindness with my words.

To my parents, you have given me so many gifts, the greatest being your unconditional love and support. I am blessed that you, two kids from the Bronx, took chances, left your comfort zones, and offered me every opportunity to pursue my goals.

Johnny Pyrch, the one, I sure am glad you called me back. Without your ability to take over and steer the beautiful ship we created, this book would still be just a dream. I'm the lucky one.

And of course to my three boys, John, Logan, and Brett, thanks for falling asleep to the light of my laptop every night. I hope I've made you proud. Never forget: Family first. Sky's the limit.

About the Author

Melissa Pyrch has been teaching high school English in New York State for over two decades. While motivating her seniors to pursue their dreams, she made a promise that she would never ask her students to do anything she wasn't willing to do herself. In that challenge, her social media account on Instagram @Pyrchgetspublished was born. She wrote this book and proved to her students that, with hard work, anything is possible.

After graduating from SUNY Cortland with a teaching certificate and a slew of sorority sisters, she landed her first teaching job. As her career evolved, she taught electives like Mass Media and Society, Poetry, Beyond the Classics, and Public Speaking. She earned a master's degree in creative writing from Manhattanville College and was named Westchester County's Cheerleading Coach of the Year. Pyrch earned an additional master's in communication arts from The College of New Rochelle where she won several academic scholarships and graduated with honors.

A highlight of her career is helping students craft college essays that reflect their truths. This experience opened her eyes to understanding the simple key to connecting with teens. Her approach: listen, acknowledge their challenges, and push them out of their comfort zones so they can fly.

While the pandemic presented an extreme challenge for educators, Pyrch was awarded June's Teacher of the Month in the Hudson Valley for her enthusiasm and ability to engage students even in a digital classroom. Most recently, she became certified in Youth Mental Health First Aid, to better support the increasing number of teens in need.

As an author, teacher, mom of three boys, and wife to a Yonkers Fire Captain, Melissa Pyrch gets to live her dream every day when the bell rings.

Stop by Instagram @Pyrchgetspublished or visit www.MelissaPyrch.com for updates and to join the fun.